Guy Rules

The Unspoken—and
Previously Unrecorded—
Rules That Govern
Men's Social Behavior

Garland H. Green, Jr.
W. P. Myers
and Dan W. Hartshorn

Andrews McMeel
Publishing
Kansas City

www.andrewsmcmeel.com

01 02 03 RDC 10 9 8 7 6 5 4

Library of Congress Cataloging-in-Publication Data

Green, Garland H.

GuyRules : the unspoken—and previously unrecorded—rules that govern men's social behavior / Garland H. Green, Jr., W. P. Myers, Dan W. Hartshorn.

p.   cm.

ISBN 0-7407-0030-8 (pbk.)

1. Men—United States—Attitudes.   2. Men—United States—Psychology.   3. Men—United States—Conduct of life.   4. Social interaction—United States.   I. Myers, W. P. (William P.)

II. Hartshorn, Dan W.   III. Title.   IV. Title: Guy rules.

HQ1090.3.G74 1999

305.31'0973—dc21   99-22163

                                                                     CIP

Design by Lee Fukui

Contents

The Rules

GUY RULES

Preface

What Is GuyRules?

Everybody always asks us: "What's GuyRules?" We've given many answers, trying to define concisely just what it is, or they are, or, well, you see what we mean. The official answer has been "a compilation of the unspoken rules that govern men's behavior." On one of our banner ads on the Web, we defined GuyRules as simply "childish and silly humor." We've found our answer changes depending on who asks. You might tell a woman, "GuyRules are all the secret rules that explain why Guys do the things they do." To the Guys you'd say something more like, "They're all the protocol we know and follow without even thinking about it." Both men and women usually smile slightly at an answer like that, but you can tell in their eyes that they don't quite understand, and an example is going to be required.

It always happens. They want to know. We always find ourselves on the spot, asked once again to give a GuyRule. Which one? There're so many. Okay, what crowd am I in? Should I pull out a gritty one for the boys, or a more politically correct, insightful tidbit for the women? Usually, we just rely on the old standbys: Driver controls the music, the Guy who tries to make the fire will stop at nothing to get it going, or the infamous urinal protocol rules.

After bathing in the wash of laughter following the telling of a couple of rules, or enduring a few seconds of silent miscomprehension, we give the lowdown on what constitutes a GuyRule: rule, insight, and humor. That's the criteria.

To be a rule, the GuyRule must be a truth about Guys that applies universally or close to it. Is it true of most Guys? Would your grandfather get it? Your neighbor on the other side of the planet?

GuyRules are very much about insight. We're not offering revelations here, simply pointing out and talking about how Guys behave and sometimes asking why. Does the rule reveal something, or further illustrate the forces behind the actions?

Finally, what's a GuyRule if it doesn't make you chuckle? First, the connection to the idea, then the flash of insight, and if all goes well, a good laugh. Face it, we can laugh at ourselves, and why not? The women do.

After we explain what GuyRules are and the conversation moves on to something else, we're left wondering if they got it and how we could explain it in just a few words next time, words that convey rule, insight, and humor all in one perfect bundle. It never quite comes together.

So until it does, we've settled for, "Well, you'll just have to get the book when it comes out next fall."

The Project That Started It All

In the spring of '95 Dan moved down to Tempe, Arizona, along with his new bride. I was excited to have him living so close to me because I had finally found a buddy to hang out with, someone who kind of liked doing the same things I did. At that time I had just purchased my first home and had begun to size up what projects I needed to complete to make it the home of my dreams. The previous home owner had done a tremendous amount of work keeping the place in great shape; however, I had plans of my own. Therefore, I set out to find and conquer my first home repair. I decide to co-opt Dan into helping me build the RV "gate of steel."

After identifying what needed to be done, I cleared the project with the wife, as every smart Guy must do, evaluated the job, saved the money, and waited for the weekend. Once it arrived, I purchased all the materials, picked up a case of beer (cans, of course), and awaited Dan's arrival. When he showed up we talked about what we were going to do, looked at the plans, and then set out to replace the "piece of junk" RV gate that was attached to the side of my house.

Once we actually started to work, we began to talk about absolutely nothing (in great detail) and I explained to Dan that I have had hundreds of these conversations and that I called them "GuyRules." We began to talk about them and found ourselves laughing at what we were doing. On a whim, I went into the house and grabbed an old pocket recorder and we began to dictate these "rules" into it. These raw thoughts would later become www.guyrules.com. The gate, on the other hand, while a wonderful design on paper, lasted a grand total of one year before falling off its hinges and

landing on the ground in a crumpled heap. Oh well, at least it was better than the junk that used to be there.

Analog to Digital to Dynamic

We only had one tape for the microrecorder, so when it filled up we'd copy it onto a bigger tape on a boom box. We'd record over the old stuff on the small tape, now safely preserved on the larger tape, if a bit scratchy. Once, the small tape was full and we hadn't got around to copying it. Gar said, "We've got to get that tape back. I have so many Guy-Rules to get down." You see, once we got started, rules started showing themselves in everything we did. We were struck with how much protocol there was and how naturally Guys just followed it.

And there it went. We transcribed GuyRules from the bigger tapes onto the computer, in digital format. Initially, we just typed them into a text document, then printed them out, one after another, just titles and rules, in the order that we put them down on tape. GuyRules then started in quasi-book format, but what it became is much different.

Around this time, the Web hit the media hard, and people were becoming aware of it. We used it to publish GuyRules and the Web site took on just as much a life of its own as GuyRules itself had. Soon we had all the rules in a database on our Linux Web server and people around the world were searching, reading, and submitting their own GuyRules. To qualify rules, or at least as an attempt to minimize the garbage we received, we created the random tests on the Web site. Guys could practice with the five-question multiple-choice quiz, which was always different and graded instantly. When they were ready, Guys could try to pass the ten-question test to receive the log-on name and password for the page, so they could submit their own GuyRule to the Web site.

We wondered if anybody would give GuyRules two seconds of their time, much less enough time to read rules, pass a test, and log in just to submit their own. But we were having so much fun playing with the Web site that we didn't care much. We'd put it all out there and see what happened.

Slowly, but steadily, Internet readers began to add to our intial collection of rules with those of their own. The first one we received from the site was "Wine Selection," and to this day, it's still one of the best rules out there. The three of us discussed over e-mail whether or not we thought a rule that came in was worthy of its place on the Web site. We got a big boost one day when Yahoo posted a link to GuyRules on their "Cool Link" page. We received thousands of visitors that day. Later, when *Maxim* magazine put a link to GuyRules on their "Fun Stuff" page, it brought us a steady flow of traffic.

Eventually, we put on-line voting tools in place to automate the process of approving, editing, and shipping GuyRules to the site. People got it. People from all over the world participated on-line and enjoyed the site. One Guy from the UK said, "Great stuff, it's all true on this side of the pond, too."

Web Power Tools for Real Guys

The Internet has played an extremely critical role in the development of GuyRules. Our Linux Web site has been an important tool. We have used it to create, polish, and display the contributions provided by participants from around the world. Without the Internet and these tools, we would not

have been able to present material of such high quality in this book.

For our grassroots-Guy effort, there is no better platform to support us than Linux, a grassroots operating system. The price was right (free) and there was in-house experience with it. Linux has been a stable platform for over two years while we developed our strategies and processes for pioneering Guydom. Some other notable tools we use on the Web site are Apache WebServer (an obvious choice), Hughes mSQL, the database in which everything is kept, and PHP, a simple scripting mechanism to get the data and put it on dynamic Web pages.

Using these tools, we individually create content from anywhere on the Internet, store it all somewhere we can all get to, present it in different ways for different tasks, and share our work with the Internet community as we do it. Even this book itself was written only using these same tools and the Web site. It allowed us to write separately or together when need be, and share our work with our editor (in another part of the world), who could provide feedback and make corrections using the Web site.

Resources (ordered by price):

> Apache http://www.apache.org
> PHP http://www.php.net
> Linux http://www.linux.org
> mSQL http://www.hughes.com.au

Rosie

So maybe we're a little gadget-centric, but that isn't really new to Guys either. The Palm Pilot, for example, was yet another way to get the word out about GuyRules. We created an application called Rosie for the popular handheld PDA to share GuyRules with more folks who wanted to read it at their leisure. Although the rules that were included with Rosie are not the ported and polished masterpieces in this book, they did help us connect with our book agent. Peter Rubie of Rubie & Perkins in New York found Rosie on the Internet and immediately got in touch with us to discuss book ideas. Rosie was, once again, the savior of the day.

theboys@guyrules.com

William P. Myers

The arrival of Bill signaled the beginning of a new era for GuyRules. Bill brought a new and much different vision to the GuyRules Web site. To Bill, the site was a virtual playground, a test bed for exploring Internet technology. He used to run a BBS (the on-line text-only predecessor to the Internet) in the early days of network computing, and the Web was really just a better version of that. Bill's expertise got the Linux Web server up and kept it up, and brought a dynamic nature to the Web site with the use of scripting tools and a database. We've had a lot of fun with the technology, and Bill always makes it seem easy.

Dan W. Hartshorn

When Dan moved to Tempe and helped work on the old RV gate, GuyRules was born. Dan's keen eye for layout and colors and his editorial and writing skills have been integral to GuyRules. A Webmaster and humorist in his own right, Dan enjoys working on all parts of the Web site, from the nuts

and bolts to the full running machine. His inner desire to be as thorough as he possibly can in everything he does has helped to make GuyRules what it is today. From the moment we all started to work together, he has demanded that we not take the easy way out to "just get it done." He has done this not with his words, but by his actions, which is as it should be in the realm of Guydom.

Garland H. Green, Jr.

Gar started GuyRules. He introduced the concept to the boys, and through the Web site, we shared it with the world. He's a continual wellspring of ideas and often comes up with creative ways to do things. Gar's talent as a painter and graphic artist has been very important to the Web site. His snappy, professional graphics are what make the look of the GuyRules Web site so cool. Gar made it possible for a site done by three Guys who hold day jobs to look like an on-going project handled by a team of developers. Gar's endless and pure inspiration is the reason GuyRules exists. His ability to think an idea through to its completion, to generate new ideas, and his writing talent have helped to bring the book from a dream to reality.

How Linux and the Internet Wrote a Book

The way GuyRules was written as a book is probably different from the way anybody has ever written a book before. We can say this with fair assurance because we know our use of technology and the Web to get things done is cutting edge. By the time the book deal landed on us, we had advanced our ability to create and use Web-based applications. They all ran on our Linux box, using Apache, mSQL, and the PHP scripting language to deliver useful applications that lived on the Web and could be accessed securely from any computer with an Internet hookup.

The first step in writing the book was to load up a database with over one hundred GuyRules that we already had and that were to be rewritten for the book. We were shooting for a certain style that we had developed with the help of our agent and our first editor. We wrote and used an application that collected each of our three separate rewrites of the rules. We could see what we were all writing, and collect the material in our database. Having this tool available on the Web served us well many times, as we could always get to it to work no matter where we were.

Once into this process, when we had enough to work with, we began meeting together to go over the individual rewrites and produce the final rule for the book. These sessions were frequent and often grueling as we worked hard to get to the pure rule, the clear insight, and find the humor that was always there in every situation we were describing. We used another application on the Web to combine these final rewrites together. Bill set up a network at his house with a Linux box that accomodated Windows and Linux workstations with a connection to the Internet. We could easily work together, or all break out and go to different workstations to mull things over on our own. In this way, we wrote the book together.

We talked our editor into using the Web to monitor our progress on the final rule rewrites and give us feedback. We stored his comments in our database and created Web pages that would show them to us. We made changes based on this

feedback—on-line, of course. Our editor logged in often and we were able to make changes as we went, and we learned how to do a better job. These tools helped us and made the process easier to handle.

On the Horizon

In this book we share the rules that we have recorded, but in the next rendition of *GuyRules: The Book*, we will share with you those rules that were submitted by other Guys from around the world. While GuyRules was begun in Tempe, Arizona, by a couple of Guys building a gate, it has become a place where men from around the world can share their thoughts on what constitutes a real man, or better yet, a real Guy.

In the writing of this book we have discovered that we can only give insight to what we have experienced. This is what makes the Web site so important. Guys from around the world have shared their insight and wisdom, creating the first chronicled collection of the mundane rules that make up our everyday life.

As we mentioned earlier these rules have passed a very rigorous process, starting with the testing procedure that must be navigated before anyone can submit a rule. When we first began this process of accepting rules from other people, we made a decision that we were not going to let just any Joe give his opinion on what makes up a GuyRule. We felt that by having an unfiltered forum in which people could just say anything, we would get just that—people saying anything.

As a result, we created a multiple-choice test that every Guy was required to pass before being given a log-in name and password, which would allow them to submit their new rule to the site. By doing so we have been able to make the submissions more uniform and true to the spirit of Guydom.

At first we felt that we would drive people away by putting an obstacle like this in front of them. When we talked to those Guys who were in our preexisting circle, they all told us that they would "never" take a test. If we wanted to get their GuyRules, they said, they "should just be allowed to give them to us" without a "stupid test."

Guys, however, being what they are, we found that they would jump straight to the test in an effort to conquer it (in most cases having never read a single GuyRule). Over a period of time, we concluded that the test taunted people into coming back for more—not to mention that the questions were clever and enjoyable to read. This is why we have included tests in the book.

For over a year the decision about whether or not to accept a rule into the club was based upon the three of us making a blind vote on if it was a "GuyRule" or "not worthy" of being a GuyRule. Many times a rule was funny, clever, and insightful but did not strike a cord with one of us. As a result, it was sent to the dungeon of "not worthy" rules, never to see the light of day again. We would contemplate and prognosticate over a rule, arguing our point of view in hopes of persuading one of the other Guys to vote it in.

It did not take long before we decided that we needed more input than just our biased opinion about rules, so we created Club Guydom. The club is a place where members can put their mark on a rule, voting it in or out as they see fit. We keep a running count of voting progress and post every vote live on the Web. With this in place we have seen the quality and quantity of rules increase. Our next book will be a compilation of the best of the best of these rules.

Acknowledgments

Dan

Thank you, Lori, for your patience and understanding throughout this process. You've been a wonderful, loving wife who has made everything easier than it might have been. My thanks goes out to John Nash, whose partnership helped us get established on the Web. Thanks to Bethe, who fed us and put up with our long nights of writing sessions. Thanks to all the Web surfers who have made the www.guyrules.com Web site all it could be. Finally, my deep thanks goes to the boys: Gar and Bill, my coauthors, who helped bring this book to life. Great job, Guys.

Gar

Thanks to my beautiful wife, Becki, who helped me write this book by giving me the strength to keep on track. You are my best friend and this could never have happened without you. To my mother, who always believed in me, even when I didn't believe in myself. Tell Kenny to put this in his pipe and smoke it. To my father, who has given me more gifts than he could ever imagine. Those gifts have been preserved in this book. To both of my sisters—you have always made me feel like a celebrity. Your belief in me has always been a source of inspiration. To Glen for sitting me down in front of Photo-Shop, and for sharing with me the stories of your life. You have given me so much. To my good buddy Harlan, who helped me understand what a GuyRule really was. You are the inspiration behind more than just "Motorcycles and New Vehicles." To Lester: the years have been a friend to you. Thanks for your kind understanding during that hard summer visit. To Marv and Pauline, who treated a young boy with respect: I will forever be thankful. To Harlow and Marline, you were my second family at a time when I desperately needed one. To Lee and Ruth: thanks for all the conversations we had while sharing more than a few cups of coffee. To my students, you continually show me the power of "going for it." Finally to Jonsey, there has never been a better friend.

Bill

I would like to thank Bethe, the tired woman behind this successful man. She kept us from killing each other during the writing of this book and I love her for it. To Eleni, Dawn, Laurynn and Shanynn, thank you for making a difference in my life. I would also like to thank my grandmother Anne, for not killing me as a child, and instead giving me a start in computers. Maybe she was hoping computers would frustrate me as much as I frustrated her. It worked.

Introduction

You'll begin your tour of Guydom with a quiz that will test how in touch you are with the true nature of Guys. After seeing where you stand, read the rules. They are divided into ten chapters by category. From "Auto" to "Wile," you'll read about the protocols for many different situations as they are naturally followed by Guys everywhere. Many of the rules are supplemented with sidebars, and there is a glossary of terms at the back of the book to allow discussions of Guydom in more detail and to clarify terminology or concepts. You'll also find a quiz question with each rule, some of them as review for what you've read, others to test you on things to come. Stay sharp and see how well you can do.

At the end of the book is the final challenge, to test your knowledge of GuyRules. Are you in balance with the forces of Guy and evil? Quiz your buddies and see how they measure up.

Book Layout

The structure of this book is intended to give you a tour of each rule. By including sidebar commentary with the rules, and including glossary terms in the back of the book, we are able to dissect every rule and approach it from many different angles. Within the rule we lay out the "correct protocol" that is used by most Guys in order to successfully navigate their way through the realm of Guydom. However, we also understand that the rule is but a reflection of what occurs naturally. It is for this reason that we have introduced the sidebars in order to interject a different point of view. This allows a Guy to react in a way other than that which the rule dictates. These different points of view are what make the rules attractive and insightful. A sidebar does not have to meet the strict standards of a GuyRule; they simply provide a place for the "yes but . . ." discussion that many rules will conjure up.

Most pages will display a "pop quiz" about a rule you have read or will read throughout the book. The intent is, first and foremost, to make the mundane sound "official" and bring legitimacy to an otherwise unofficial event. By doing so, we know we indirectly poke fun at ourselves. By providing a test question on every page, we cue you to look for certain pieces of content that are scattered throughout the book. You will want to pay close attention to the test questions, because there will be a test at the end of the book. It is this test that will give you access to the section of the www.guyrules.com Web site where you can publish your own GuyRule for the entire world to read.

Final Exam

How well do you think you know Guys? Do you know who calls breaks on a project? Who controls the radio in the car? When you must avoid the fortune cookie? Test your knowledge of Guydom to see where you stand.

Do you know what to do in every situation? What your buddy would do? GuyRules sheds light on the finer details of protocol. Did you learn everything you need to know? Fortunately, the test will inform you about whether or not you're equipped with everything you need to navigate through the realm of Guydom. Now go forth and be a Guy.

Visit www.guyrules.com to post your test score, join Club Guydom, and submit your own GuyRules.

Glossary Terms

Much of this book states the obvious about what Guys already know. We've put glossary terms in the book to increase understanding by defining the elements that make up most Guys.

Some terms are used to describe situations that are common among Guys, like a "quick-click look." In other instances, glossary terms are used to describe other parts of our lives, like Grilldom or Camperatus. GuyRules has a lingo all its own. It's Guybonics.

Entrance
Exam

1. When going for a beer, what is the big let-me-into-the-club-early kind of move?

   A. handing the other Guy the first beer
   B. getting someone a beer without asking them if they wanted one
   C. asking them first if they want a beer
   D. giving them the better beer

2. When you're at your buddy's house and you feel the urge to adjust his stereo:

   A. make sure you have the right remote
   B. play it safe, don't use a remote
   C. ask his wife how to use his stereo
   D. don't even think of it, that's his territory
   E. ask for his permission first

3. Guys must be loyal to their products. Once a Guy's been using a brand of something for a while:

   A. he'll stick to it and swear by it
   B. he will know every place to buy it
   C. he'll act like a salesman hawking it to all his buddies
   D. he will tell his wife to only buy that brand

4. When you're trying to keep up with your buddy, you should not be too hard on yourself because:

   A. you're not in as bad shape as you think
   B. over time it doesn't matter
   C. your buddy is doing all that to try and impress you anyway
   D. your buddy is your buddy and he doesn't care

5. When smoking a cigar for the first time, you:

A. follow the lead of the other Guys

B. act perfectly comfortable, like you've done this a million times

C. annoy as many people as possible

D. turn it around backward in your mouth and blow smoke at your buddies

6. Should you eat the last piece of pizza with a group of Guys?

A. why not?

B. never, respect for the kill is vital

C. only if you had less than everyone else

D. yes, then throw the box across the room

7. There is only a maximum of two "accidental" leg incursions before:

A. you start telling the Guy off

B. you tell your buddy about the Guy next to you

C. you think of kicking this Guy's butt

D. one of the Guys starts to get nervous

8. The Guy riding shotgun is responsible for:

A. making sure that the music is loud

B. making sure no good-looking babe goes unnoticed

C. food inventory and distribution

D. all the direction navigation

9. **You must weave your web of distortion to prove that no other man could have:**

   A. ever beaten you if you were sober
   B. ever been so mad as you were then
   C. done any better in the same situation
   D. beaten the other Guy

10. **Every Guy must avoid the self-imposed pressure of:**

   A. new gear expectations
   B. following the hard-to-use directions
   C. performing on his anniversary
   D. the old girlfriend meeting the new girlfriend
   E. answering quizzes correctly

5. correct answer: B   10. correct answer: A
4. correct answer: C   9. correct answer: C
3. correct answer: A   8. correct answer: C
2. correct answer: D   7. correct answer: D
1. correct answer: B   6. correct answer: B

Chapter 1

Auto

GUY AUTO

Cars are the one thing we all are supposed to know about, but usually don't, and usually don't let on that we don't. It may be repair, navigation, driving skill, or just general presentation, but our status in Guydom is often reflected through our vehicles. The types of cars themselves allude to gender differences, and any Guy can distinguish a woman's car from a man's car on sight. Whereas women tend to go for the more practical, men tend to use other criteria. Most men don't have a problem justifying a Lamborghini that can do 150 miles per hour. In fact, for Guys it's very practical. We're often so far behind for appointments that we need to go 150 miles per hour to make them on time, hence making it very practical.

Trucks are also a big part of automotive manhood. This stems from early childhood, where most likely a fire truck or dump truck was given as a gift, setting goals and expectations at a young age. As we grow older the level of sophistication does not necessarily increase, just the size. As grown men, our goals aren't much different than they were as boys. We just want bigger trucks, with power windows and, of course, a V-8, rather than settling for flashing headlights and authentic digitized truck sounds. Batteries are included in the full-size versions, making them even more marketable to

the already savvy "batteries not included" shoppers. Of course, "assembly required" still holds its appeal.

Repair is also a large aspect of the Guy's playing field. There are a number of reasons why Guys like this dirty, knuckle-bustin', frustrating affair. For one thing, when repairs go awry, it gives us a good excuse to cuss and throw things around. Besides, it is one of the few ways that Guys get to score bargaining chips with the wife. In addition, it also gives us an excuse to hang out in the garage, which is yet another good excuse for using that old TV that's out there, which is actually just another excuse for finishing the beer that's out there as well. The alcohol doesn't really help sharpen one's skills for the main activities, like the repair itself, which explains much of the knuckle-busting aspect of working on cars. Nevertheless, it is repeated by countless men every Sunday.

Automotive Knowledge

Guys must never reveal their *true* level of automotive knowledge (or lack thereof). They never comment during unfamiliar repairs to avoid risking "automotive knowledge exposure." Rather, they wait for a safe opportunity to share what little knowledge they do have, in order to act like they know what the hell they're talking about. Outwardly ridicule but secretly respect the Guy who can actually stand up defiantly and say, "Now, classical music is one thing, but I don't know jack-shit about cars."

SIDEBAR

 In the event that you find yourself being grilled by a buddy about how to fix something on his car, simply note the make and model, and explain that you only know how to fix the older models.

Blue Minivan Pass

A Guy never lets a woman in a light blue minivan pass him on the freeway. Never. Even if all he's got under the hood is a four cylinder with 113,000 miles, he'll stop at nothing short of throwing a rod before he lets her pass. This applies to other colors as well. Black minivans with tinted windows are okay because they're probably CIA or FBI. Let 'em go.

SIDEBAR

If you're ever in the unfortunate position of having to drive a blue minivan for somebody, make the best of it by trying to pass all the Guys you see on the freeway. But be careful not to get caught up in an ego-feedback loop that ends up causing you to break state speeding records.

POP QUIZ

When someone from your buddy's team receives a good hit from your team, you:

- **A.** give him hell by offering to take his team out for ice cream if they win
- **B.** insist that it should have been called by the refs
- **C.** acknowledge the good hit
- **D.** claim it was a lucky shot and that he'd better watch out next time
- **E.** just sit and take all the crap your buddy can dish out

Different Sets of Directions

Guys have two sets of directions that they give: (1) The this-would-be-hard-for-somebody-else-to-find directions, or (2) You're-a-total-dumbass-if-you-can't-follow-these directions.

Directions pressure: When a Guy's girlfriend asks for directions in front of his buddies, he's under an immense amount of pressure to give clear and correct directions. Then every Guy there must give his own, better directions.

POP QUIZ

The true master of the TV channel-surf is the Guy who can flash back to his show:

- **A.** just as it's fading back into the scene
- **B.** while holding a beer in one hand and a sandwich in the other
- **C.** and not miss a beat, but still stay on top of the sports scores
- **D.** A and C

Driver Controls the Music

The driver controls the radio. As a passenger, you can make a token protest, in the hope that you might prevent being sucked into the black hole of listening to your buddy's music all the time. But the driver still controls the radio.

If need be, strong-arm your music into the song rotation, particularly if you are going to be riding with this Guy for a while. There is nothing more painful than carpooling and getting stuck listening to his music. If you find yourself looking for a CD of his songs, you have a serious problem.

POP QUIZ

Initiating the hello when you're walkin' past a Guy on the sidewalk is:

- **A.** a good idea
- **B.** just a nice thing to do
- **C.** like staging for a drag race
- **D.** not needed; just shut up and walk

Driving with Fast Food

Every Guy must be skilled in the art of driving while eating fast food. The Guy riding shotgun is responsible for food inventory and distribution. Your ability to eat while driving with your leg, opening catsup with your teeth, and dipping fries is one of the most respected driving skills.

SIDEBAR

There are few things better than driving and eating a full meal without getting chow all over the front of your shirt. Every Guy has received at least one catsup battle scar while eating and driving.

POP QUIZ

Each major piece of clothing must pass:

- **A.** your wife's strict standards
- **B.** the "matching test"
- **C.** the "sniff test"
- **D.** your strict standards

Grinding the Gears

The ability to shift gears smoothly and aggressively is one of the true measures of Guydom. If you grind a gear, that's it: dumb Guy. Fight the instinct to look around to see who saw you grind. It's a dead giveaway.

SIDEBAR

 If the grind occurs during a demonstration of your ability to speed shift, it is acceptable to use any excuse that proves that you are not comfortable with speed shifting, because on a normal basis, you don't abuse your cars. Make sure that your buddy knows you were just demonstrating the technique.

POP QUIZ

When talking to your pets with your buddies around, you should:

- **A.** talk softly and intimately so your buddies can see your nurturing side
- **B.** address your pets in formal tongue only
- **C.** talk to the dog only and protest about the cats
- **D.** real men only have aquariums, and fish don't mind how you talk to them

Hands off the Environment

The Guy driving the car adjusts the temperature and the direction of the vents. It's a complete breach of etiquette for the passenger to adjust the vents. Many a tense moment has passed when the Guy riding shotgun was sweating his ass off, waiting anxiously for his buddy to think of his boy.

SIDEBAR

A guy would rather be down two weeks with the flu than admit to his buddy that he's uncomfortable.

SIDEBAR

God rest his soul if the other Guy has to remind him in a bloody sweat to think of him.

POP QUIZ

When a bachelor leaves clothes in the washer too long, and his shirts develop a musty smell, he cannot:

- **A.** wear a rotting shirt when he's going out on a first date
- **B.** tell his buddies about it
- **C.** keep smelling the shirt all day
- **D.** just rewash the load without considering whether or not he can get away with the stink

How Fast?

Every Guy has a mental speedometer in his head that records the fastest he's ever been in a car, to the exact mile per hour. When hanging with the boys, you have to throw out your "how fast" speed as if it were a challenge. As with the "longest-fish story," the speed will increase as the years go by.

SIDEBAR

When you are with your buddy and he launches into his "how fast" story, and you notice he is kicking up the speed, never let on that you know he is not telling the truth, especially if you were in the car with him. Because you rode with him, you have a "post facto" speed addition to your own story.

P O P   Q U I Z

When you go to break up with a woman, where should you *not* do it?

- **A.** during the last two minutes of a football game
- **B.** her family reunion (that way she's got a support network)
- **C.** go out for some egg rolls and tell her at the restaurant
- **D.** at the movies
- **E.** do it on a Monday; they couldn't get worse no matter what you do

Jockey for Position

While in most aspects of driving a little competition is expected, in a traffic jam the Guy who cuts everyone off just to gain a couple of car lengths looks like an ass. You can only make up to three lane changes before giving up and sticking to one lane. There is no need to fight traffic just to switch lanes and move from behind a Guy to beside the same Guy.

SIDEBAR

It is acceptable to fight your way past a Guy in the heaviest of traffic if he is riding on or tapping the brakes.

POP QUIZ

Why would you get demoted to gofer on a project?

- **A.** you brought cheap beer in bottles to the project
- **B.** you didn't have your own tools to bring to the project
- **C.** you really stink at hammering
- **D.** same as above and you can't use a handsaw either

Let Him In

When you are driving and another Guy needs to merge into your lane, by all means let him in. Don't act like you're in the draft at Talladega, and that by letting him merge you would lose the Winston Cup championship. If you are the Guy that was let in, don't be a jerk. Give the other Guy the hand-wave acknowledgment for tossing you the merging bone.

SIDEBAR

When a Guy gives you the hand-wave acknowledgment, be sure to reciprocate with your own wave so he knows you saw him.

POP QUIZ

Every time you finish a large home-improvement project, it's imperative that you:

- **A.** keep the receipts for a tax write-off
- **B.** pretend that it really didn't cost that much
- **C.** start planning for the next one
- **D.** drag every single human being through the gory project details

Motorcycles and New Vehicles

When your buddy gets a new vehicle, it is required that you say something nice about it. However, if you just can't stomach that new '86 Ford Taurus, just mention something trivial about how great the radio knobs are, or perhaps the map pockets. That way, you fulfill your Guydomal obligation with the "purchase approval," while sending the subtle message that the vehicle really sucks.

SIDEBAR

 Try to be honest in your assessment; chances are the Guy is having buyer's remorse since he's stuck with his purchase for a while. Offer sound financial advice on the Guy's purchase only before he buys the vehicle. After he's purchased it, he owns that baby for a while and doesn't want you giving him your Monday-morning breakdown.

POP QUIZ

Every Guy has his "I-beat-the-sales-Guy" story when he buys a truck or car, but he will never:

- **A.** tell his buddies how much he really paid
- **B.** admit to paying too much for an extended warranty
- **C.** have an I-beat-the-saleswoman story
- **D.** admit he has bad credit and paid too high an interest rate

On Pumping Gas

Guys have a technique that'll get that last hoseful of gas out of the pump and into their car. You don't just let the pump stop, pull the hose, and be done with it. There is that shake-squeeze, the handle-rattle-hose method that will get you that last little bit of gas that you may have otherwise missed if you didn't know the "secret."

SIDEBAR

While you may have your own technique for getting that last little bit of gas into your car, whatever you do, don't spill gas on the side of the car or on your clothes. Your goal is to get as much gas into the car as possible, so be sure to avoid the "dribble" before hanging up the hose.

POP QUIZ

Every Guy must laugh when his buddy gets hit in the testicles because:

    A. his buddy is about to puke

    B. it only happens every once in a while

    C. all Guys have experienced this dreaded event

Parking

Guys must be adept at threading the parking needle. Nothing is worse than showing up at the party and doing a thirteen-point turn into a parallel park with all your buddies standing around on the lawn, beers in hand. Man and machine are most as one when moving less than five miles per hour, and nowhere is this more apparent than in the display of a Guy's parking prowess.

SIDEBAR

Every Guy falls into a "parking slump" every once in a while. Just hang in there and keep at it. Don't think twice about your buddy's snide comments about how far you are away from the curb or how many times you backed out and then in to try to make the turn into a parking spot.

POP QUIZ

When your buddy asks you if you got laid on your date:

- **A.** tell him that it's none of his business and to get a life
- **B.** ask him when was the last time he made visual contact with any member of the female race
- **C.** crack open a beer and give him all the gory details
- **D.** make up a wild story about it, regardless of what really happened
- **E.** what you do depends completely on your level of respect for your date

Talking to the Mechanic

Whenever you question a car mechanic about your repair, you must act like you actually know just what the heck the Guy is saying once he starts telling you. Be subtle, though–if your eyes start to glaze over he might test you by throwing out a term like "iscandarian rollalugnut" to see if you just keep nodding.

POP QUIZ

You've gotta wear your most expensive, very special cologne:

A. when you want to signify that you're on an official date

B. when you did not take a shower

C. when your buddy is wearing his special stuff

D. when you're using the same bottle that you still have from three girlfriends ago

Unintentional Start

Never make the mistake of "starting" your already running car. Short of grinding your gears, there is no worse automotive offense. If you do try to fire up your ride with the engine running, be a good sport while your buddies render their judgment. Never let your wife hear you do it, because every time she does it, you'll have to sit there and keep your mouth shut.

SIDEBAR

When confronted with the sharp reality of metal grinding metal during the unintentional start, you must be willing to accept full responsibility for your stupid action. However, if you can in some way pawn it off on a quiet-running car, do it.

POP QUIZ

Why do you mismatch your plates when your buddy comes over for dinner?

A. to irritate him
B. to make him feel more comfortable
C. because you don't know any better
D. because all your dishes are dirty

You Didn't Really Almost Get into an Accident

If you find yourself in a "driving situation" in which you know you just barely escaped an accident, you must act like you were in complete control of the entire event. Quickly divert attention to the road conditions or the other car's driver. Hopefully there will be some wildlife around that you can blame as well, but *never* admit you almost got into an accident.

SIDEBAR

 When driving with the wife, do not make reference to the fact that the other car's driver was a woman—this can lead to the "riot act."

SIDEBAR

 It Is imperative that you be able to outline your case to the wife, citing specific examples from the situation most favorable to your case.

POP QUIZ

When a project goes bad, every Guy must:

- **A.** blame the other Guy for the failure
- **B.** stop and discuss at length who and what went bad
- **C.** stop and get a beer before fixing it
- **D.** call in an expert to fix it

GUY RULES

Chapter 2
Buddies

GUY BUDDIES

Many humorous insights into our behavior are revealed in the interactions between buddies. A Guy's group of pals is practically sacred to him. After all, your buddies are the ones who support you with scathing sarcasm, assist you by pointing out your mistakes, and keep you honest and true to Guydom by letting you know when you're being an idiot. When you're down, you can count on a good buddy to throw you a bone or give you an out. When you're up, your buddies will be there to party in your honor and make sure you feel it the next morning.

Behavior among buddies is less formal, but often more complex than the protocol between strangers. We always develop customary rules with our buddies, known only to the group, which are followed at least as closely as more general protocol. We all have our inside jokes, secret codes, and signals that are collected over time and used to communicate in very subtle ways.

Always stick by your buddies and don't forget how important they are. Who else is going to listen to you complain about your job or your woman? Who else will keep you out all night and get you in trouble? Who better to give you unsolicited advice, make smart-ass comments, or share in the fat? Our buddies will always help us carry the load, no matter how far or how heavy.

Acknowledging a Good Toss

When you throw something to a buddy, be it ball, beer, or babe, you must acknowledge the good catch. That must be returned with an immediate "Nice throw." A good catch not acknowledged is like a good throw not made. In this way, Guys play catch with compliments.

SIDEBAR

 Tossing something across a distance to another Guy is one of the most basic skills any Guy must possess. Even if you can't throw well, you get respect points from your buddies by giving it your best. But you know the next thing they'll toss around is your battered ego.

POP QUIZ

If your wife or girlfriend decides that she wants to jump out of a plane, bungee jump, or some other crazy thing:

- **A.** tell her to go for it, you'll cheer her on
- **B.** make up a good excuse to get out of doing it
- **C.** try to talk her out of it
- **D.** you must participate as well
- **E.** dump her and move on to safer ground

Carrying Your Load

When you're physically carrying something with a buddy, you have to be willing to carry your fair share of the load. You must act like the load is not as heavy as it may appear. If you're not able to keep up with your buddy, initiate the "new grip" ploy to buy yourself some time. Never show strain or let on that you are about to drop dead if you have to carry the load one more step.

SIDEBAR

 Avoid at all costs having to make more than one grip adjustment. The Guy on the other end is probably about to drop dead as well, so don't make these fake adjustments unless you need them.

Cigars: The Ultimate Guy Occasion

Cigar smoking is the perfect Guy event. Being outwardly comfortable with a big stinky weed on fire five inches in front of your face is pure Guydom.

SIDEBAR

Every Guy must attempt to get all the nuances of the ritual right. Rookies will sometimes bite off the end of one that didn't need it and smile proudly at you with tobacco on his lips and in his teeth; or describe the character of the smoke and pretend like he knows what constitutes a good cigar.

When "assembly required" comes up in a new purchase, what should you do?

  A. don't read the documentation but just look at the pictures
  B. take as much time as needed to carefully read the documentation so you don't look foolish later
  C. read the "tools required" list so you know what to get off the Peg-Board tool holder
  D. establish early that you got a few extra pieces, and some might be left over at the end

Did You Get Laid?

When your buddy comes back from a night out with a new woman, you always have to ask him if he got laid. If he respects her, he will reply that he didn't get laid, whether he did or not. If he doesn't respect her, he will reply that he got laid, whether he did or not. The truth is irrelevant.

SIDEBAR

 Most Guys are tempted to go down the "trumpet my exploits" road and betray their dates to their buddies. When you do resist and refuse to answer one way or the other, it's open season on you, and your buddies will start taunting you about the wedding, the six kids, and the end to your control over your life.

SIDEBAR

 Spare your buddies the details of your performance, unless of course your sick little band of friends is into that. Just don't send us postcards about it.

POP QUIZ

When secretly rating another Guy on his lumber selection:

    A. cover up your own mistakes
    B. blame a low rating on the store
    C. ask your wife for help
    D. only point out errors with your closest buddies
    E. let the Guy do his job

Different Good-byes

Guy-byes. Level one, some Guy: quick handshake with an even quicker "Hey, have a nice life. Nice knowing ya." Level two, coworker: handshake, a shoulder squeeze, or a pat on the back. Level three, party Guy: handshake, hug, and a quick couple of grunts. Level four, lifelong buddy: roll up your sleeves and grab him like you would your wife. (Rarely seen in males outside captivity.)

SIDEBAR

Observe a man at one of his most emotionally exposed moments, when he must say good-bye to his good buddy. His quick, choppy actions and feeble attempts at sarcasm are clues to the Guy within, but that's nothing compared to the eyes. You'll never see true eye contact occurring. This is done as a defensive measure.

POP QUIZ

When eating fast food and driving, the Guy riding shotgun is responsible for:

- **A.** food inventory and distribution
- **B.** making sure that he pays for the food
- **C.** holding the sodas while you drive
- **D.** commenting on the Guy working in the drive-through

Giving Your Buddy an Out

When you're working with a buddy and it comes to the point when you know he screwed up, and he knows he screwed up, you must give your buddy an out. The simplicity of the common male is most easily recognized in the cornered animal. Giving him an out lets him off the hook, and reminds him that next time, he must give you an out. A Guy doesn't let his buddies flounder.

SIDEBAR

It's one thing to give your buddy an out and it's another thing to absolve him of his mess. Don't go soft or anything. Acceptable examples of "outs" include: There's a knot in that wood; That dude cut you off; The grass is slick, anyone could have fallen on their ass; I would've puked on the bar too if I'd eaten that many jalapeño poppers; It's a tough course; Hey, you haven't played in weeks; By next year, her parents won't even remember how your car looked flipped over on their front lawn.

SIDEBAR

If you see your buddy spinning out of control, toss him the lifeline he needs and say something that can get him out his self-imposed jam.

Starting a fire today is a return to primeval Guydom because:

- **A.** we are all plagued by the pyro-bug
- **B.** fire was the start of GuyRules
- **C.** we don't have to light a fire to cook
- **D.** it's always been the wife's job to cook

Guy Scar-Offs

A Guy must compete for the biggest scar and the most painful story. The Guy with the ugliest scar coupled with the most grotesque story will win the "scar-off" Olympics. Those unable to embellish must withdraw from the competition and enjoy the show.

SIDEBAR

Never make an unsubstantiated surgical claim about the scar unless you are willing to back it up with anatomical facts to support your claim. There is nothing worse than finding yourself engaged in a conversation with another Guy who had the same injury but knows medical stuff to back it up.

POP QUIZ

If you're going to take a drink off your buddy's beer, you must:

- **A.** never let the bottle touch your lips
- **B.** avoid backsplash by applying a certain technique
- **C.** chug the whole beer to prove your manhood
- **D.** pretend you like it, even if you hate that brand
- **E.** only take a small drink to respect your buddy

Helping Your Buddy Leave

When hanging out with a buddy at your place, you must be willing to help him leave, so he can come over and play again some other night. Give him a look that acknowledges the fact that he is going to get chewed out by the wife when he gets home. Let him know that he has fulfilled his requirement to stay long enough to "prove" that he is in control of his woman.

SIDEBAR

 If for some reason your buddy does not quite grasp the fact that you have his best interest in mind, pretend that you are the one that wants him to leave so you can go to bed. Be willing to blow him off for his own good.

POP QUIZ

If your buddy is complaining about his weight, you can make him feel better by:

- **A.** reassuring him that he's not that fat
- **B.** agreeing with him and ridiculing him
- **C.** sharing the fat, by saying you're fat too
- **D.** complimenting his wife's cooking

I Beat the Sales Guy

Every Guy has his "I-beat-the-sales-Guy" story from when he bought his truck or car. No Guy, on the other hand, has an "I-beat-the-saleswoman" story.

SIDEBAR	
	Be prepared to be asked how much you paid for your new ride. If you are asked, you can pretend that you don't remember how much you finally paid after you got your rebate. You only have to admit how much you pay per month. Never tell how much you got for your trade, because chances are you got boned anyway.
SIDEBAR	
	You must never let on that you have no clue what a car really costs. No matter how much you may want to think you got a good deal, there will always be another Guy who got a better one.

POP QUIZ

If you're going out with the boys, tell the wife:

- **A.** that you're going to the store to pick up some things
- **B.** some made-up story to mask your true intent
- **C.** at the last possible moment
- **D.** you'll be back soon, even though you both know it'll be late
- **E.** you're going out and that's that

Introducing a Buddy to New Terminology

Guys often flex their intellectual muscles by introducing their buddies to new terminology. This must be met with various affirmations in order to validate a Guy's terminology. Guys may secretly question this new terminology, but they wait for the privacy of their own personal embarrassment before checking it out.

SIDEBAR

Of course, there's always one buddy who refuses to be impressed. His refusal to comply can be dangerous, shaking up the entire balance of Guydom. This is usually the Guy who doesn't actually know much of anything himself, and survives social circles on sheer ego alone.

POP QUIZ

When is it acceptable to fart in another Guy's car?

- **A.** anytime
- **B.** only after a long road trip
- **C.** only after he himself has farted
- **D.** when you think you can get away with it

Listening In

Guys never listen in on their buddy's phone conversations. It is incumbent on the Guy whose wife is on the line to take the call in another room, so that his buddies won't realize just how little control he has over his "kingdom." Unless they're old pals, in which case, of course, they'll already know.

SIDEBAR	
	A common technique used to discreetly leave the room is to pace around with the phone, making longer and longer advances toward the next room until you slip out unnoticed. If you do a good job at it, your buddies might not hassle you too much for slinking away to be sweet with your woman in private.
SIDEBAR	
	Some Guys opt for the macho approach: He'll speak louder than necessary and parade the conversation in front of his friends. This tough ploy saves him a lot of face with his buddies, perhaps even gains him respect, but rest assured it will backfire once he gets home and suddenly his pals don't see him for a month.

POP QUIZ

If a Guy isn't sure his woman is cool with him having porn, he must:

- **A.** hide it forever and always
- **B.** give it away to his buddies
- **C.** confront her with it and insist that she get into it
- **D.** send out a porn tracer to test the waters

Most Famous Person

Every Guy must have his "I met a famous person" story, and the amount of respect received from your buddies is proportional to how famous the person is. Sometimes it's really pathetic how obscure the connection to actual fame is. Vicarious connections to not-so-famous people are not looked upon favorably.

POP QUIZ

When you are driving and another Guy needs to merge into your lane, don't:

- **A.** speed up to cut him off
- **B.** flip him off if he cuts in front of you
- **C.** act like you're in the draft at Talladega
- **D.** swerve and act like you almost got hit

Porn Anticipation

A Guy can't leave his buddy hanging with "porn anticipation." If he tells his buddy he's going to swap tapes, he has to follow through, and not leave his buddy hanging the weekend his wife is out of town.

POP QUIZ

If you promise your buddy that you'll bring over new porn for him to borrow the weekend his wife is away:

A. you must ask him to return it after the weekend

B. ask him later if he watched it

C. never leave him hanging by not coming over after all

D. bring a kid's movie that's labeled *Hot Babes in Barbados* as a joke

E. give him the porn, then keep calling him all night so he can't enjoy it

Reacting to Your Buddy Getting Hit in the Nuts

Every Guy must laugh when his buddy gets hit in the testicles. All Guys have experienced this dreaded event and know the difference between the "light-brush-bead-sweat" and the official, full-blown hit in the balls.

P O P   Q U I Z

When you're drinking the hard stuff and it hits you wrong:

   A. spit it up and laugh at yourself
   B. grimace and howl
   C. hit it again to wash it down
   D. show no expression and say, "Ah, that's good"

She's Cool with It

A Guy never admits to his buddies that he's in any way under the control of his wife. When the time comes to party with the boys, Guys never admit to one another that their wives really *do* mind that they're going out. Instead, a Guy will confidently say, "Oh, she's cool with it!" while wondering how many chick flicks he'll have to watch to pay for this night out.

POP QUIZ

When a Guy realizes another Guy is talking a bunch of crap, it's acceptable to:

    A. ask him to explain himself better

    B. trump his bullshit flat out because it is expected practice between Guys

    C. wait until he leaves the room before saying anything

    D. go along with whatever he says and act like he is cool

    E. just blow it off because he is your buddy

Smart-Ass Comments

Some Guys work in smart-ass comments like some women work in guilt. They come in varying degrees, depending on how far you are into a project, or how well you know the Guy. Early on you might really fuck with a Guy, but later in the project smart-ass comments must be administered sparingly due to the fact that the Guy is going to go postal on you for taunting him. This is particularly true if you are heavy on the smart-ass comments at the beginning.

SIDEBAR	
	A smart-ass comment is an art form in itself, and those who are blessed with the gift are highly respected by other Guys. Their buddies, however, are not so blessed, as they have to put up with this Guy all the time.
SIDEBAR	
	Usually, the degree to which smart-ass comments are used corresponds directly to the degree to which Guys know one another. They're always judging at what level of acceptance the other Guy is, so they can loosen up and drop the politeness.

Token Protests

Every Guy must employ the token protest at least once before relinquishing control of a situation. If a Guy's really working hard, like he's been hauling furniture or hanging drywall all day, any good buddy will notice signs of fatigue and offer to help, or even take over. At this point, the Guy must use at least one token protest before he can pass along the duty with relief and catch his breath. Of course, it's a total breach of etiquette if the buddy accepts the token protest at face value and leaves the Guy half dead to keep busting his ass.

SIDEBAR

By natural instinct, the Guy will toss out the token protest, "Naw, no thanks, I'm fine." Understanding the order of things, his buddy will return, "You sure? I don't mind at all, without, of course, alluding to the fact that it looks like the Guy's about to fall over dead.

Unsolicited Advice

Generally, unsolicited advice is not welcome in the realm of Guydom, particularly early on in a fix-it project. Nobody likes the "early-jumper-in Guy." A Guy has to let his buddy fumble around until either he asks for advice or the Guy just can't stand to watch his buddy screw up for one more second. By jumping in too early, a Guy risks throwing the whole project into chaos. He might just as well walk up to his buddy and ask him if he failed wood shop and took home economics instead.

SIDEBAR

If your buddy keeps jumping in too early to try to "help" you "fix" your problem, don't respond with the weak "Well fine then, you do it." Instead, do what he says, but keep making little mistakes to really annoy him. He'll get the idea.

Chapter 3
Ego

GUY EGO

It is not surprising that this is a large category in this book, as it offers an excellent gauge to the reverent size of ego in Guydom. This is a preoccupation with something more stealthy than today's most advanced military hardware, and we will protect and defend it with no less tenacity than the military (see "guerrilla ego"). The balance that we have to maintain between our egos and what we know to be reality is often difficult and riddled with mistakes.

One might assume that we keep our well-preened egos in shape to impress the opposite sex like a peacock in full bloom, but as is often the case, they come into play more during a Guy's interaction with other Guys. Women are, and have been, fully aware of this whole ego thing from the start, and have been able to put it into perspective with men. Guys, on the other hand, continue to misread and react to poorly gathered information, leading to some ruffled feathers at times.

The ego serves as our protective shield in homophobic situations, where men need to establish that they're men. This seemingly simple task turns out to be, for a lot of Guys, a full-time job. Homophobic tactics and displays are endlessly repeated and understood by all Guys. Whether it is simply acknowledging another Guy's presence or recovering from knee-to-knee contact, we are constantly trying to establish our place in the ego-asylum.

Initiating the Hello

Initiating the hello when you're walkin' past a Guy on the sidewalk is like staging for a drag race: neither one wants to pull up to the line first. When at all possible, utter the first hello for the sake of getting on with the race, thus maintaining a solid balance of Guydom.

SIDEBAR

Guys passing each other on the street never communicate directly, but greet each other in the most subtle way possible. It's less a greeting, really, than an acknowledgment of each other's existence. It avoids a confrontation due to lack of mutual respect. Techniques include the slight head nod, the quick head jerk, or brief eye contact accompanied by a terse "Heh." Don't walk past a Guy and say, "Hi there, lovely day, isn't it?" It's impossible to predict what the outcome would be of such a gross breach of etiquette.

POP QUIZ

Your buddy's better off making a pass at your wife than firing up your grill:

A. true

B. false

Armrest Control in the Movie Theater

While at the movies and sitting next to some other Guy, the chair's armrest becomes the battleground. Lose some battles if necessary, but win the war. Only give it up to maintain a solid balance of Guydom.

SIDEBAR

 Never take the elbow and physically force the other Guy's arm off the armrest. You must be able to successfully position the elbow as far back as possible by making small tactical adjustments that are almost unnoticeable. This can last as long as the movie is playing; however, it is best to establish control and then relinquish it halfway through the movie, just to toss the other Guy a bone.

POP QUIZ

The lowest echelon of burp is done by the Guy who sucks air into his gut and:

- **A.** tries to pretend it was real
- **B.** blows it into your face
- **C.** continues to burp even when he doesn't have to
- **D.** spells words like "bullshit" with the burp

Cling-Ons

When a Guy gets out of the water, it is vital that he pull the bathing suit away from his now shrunken crotch. Unless, of course, he has a huge penis and an ego to match; then he'll definitely display that. At the swimming pool, avoid the ladder, because it will make the needed adjustment much more difficult to execute covertly.

SIDEBAR

You must be skilled in the ability to get the suit as far away from "Mr. Happy" as possible without seeming paranoid about the less-than-stellar state of affairs.

POP QUIZ

When you buy new gear for that competitive sport you play with your buddies:

- **A.** warn them of their impending doom at the hands of your new gear
- **B.** don't wear all of it at once or everybody will think you're a dork
- **C.** run over it a few times with the truck to naturalize it
- **D.** mask your purchase with silence--the new gear is intimidation enough
- **E.** solicit compliments from your buddies to validate your purchase

Do It Yourself!

Any project or repair that a Guy can possibly do by himself or for himself is done that way. Guys should not seek advice unless they've exhausted all their personal resources. Guys are more stubborn than stupid, so to show what they can do, they do it themselves. This helps explain the natural aversion to the early-jumper-in Guy. Every Guy has a god-given right to *do it himself.*

SIDEBAR

You can, however, find ways to trick other Guys into doing work for you if it suits your selfish needs.

When you're hanging around in your buddy's house, should you adjust his stereo?

- **A.** sure, he'd understand
- **B.** only if the music he has on really sucks
- **C.** if he's in the other room, it's okay
- **D.** not if you value your life

Elevator Buttons

Every Guy has to push the elevator button for himself, even if it's already lit. You can't let another Guy operate a piece of "shared" machinery for you. Under no circumstances does a Guy allow a woman to push the buttons for him. That would remove the chance of the preliminary check-out a Guy is afforded while asking her, "What floor?"

SIDEBAR	
	It's also okay to select the next floor above or below her choice to get a better look.

SIDEBAR	
	For some reason, Guys find themselves pushing the already lighted buttons like some electronic placebo, as if by magic *their* push might be the one to get them to their destination.

POP QUIZ

Some Guys try to be like Mighty Casey on steroids in some:

   A. cartoon from the twenties

   B. Saturday-morning TV show

   C. neanderthal flashback

   D. attempt to act like the Babe

Every Guy Has a Get-Rich Scheme

Every Guy has his own get-rich scheme that nobody else has ever thought of. Of course, you can't just go out and tell everybody about it. Most Guys don't even tell their wives. They're afraid the old lady's gonna shoot it down. If your buddy lets you in on his top-secret get-rich-quick scheme, that means something: that's a GuyBond.

SIDEBAR

Some Guys seem to come up with the dumbest ideas and end up telling everyone. They seem to believe in their idea almost to an extreme. Some of these Guys will actually get an idea to market. Suddenly they go from dreamer to visionary in 2.5 seconds once money changes hands, and then everyone wants on board.

POP QUIZ

As with the "longest-fish story," your "how fast" speed will increase as:

- **A.** the years go by
- **B.** you tell the story to different people
- **C.** long as no one can verify your lie
- **D.** you keep it within reason

Fat Etiquette

Don't reach over and grab another Guy's love handles. That's reserved for his wife. You wouldn't want another Guy grabbin' your flab. The exception might be with the longtime, totally-know-the-Guy buddy. But in that case, be prepared to share the fat (see "Sharing of the Fat," page 192).

(see "Sharing of the Fat," page 192)

SIDEBAR

So if you walk up to a Guy and you say, "How're ya doin', Joe," and grab his big fat gut, that's a total breach of etiquette.

SIDEBAR

You have to respect the Guy who grabs his own gut, wraps both hands around it, and shakes it like an overfilled water balloon. That is the ultimate in sharing the fat.

POP QUIZ

If you decide to dye your hair blond, you should:

A. get the best quality dye for better results

B. consult with your wife on the procedure

C. do it yourself, never trust anyone else with the job

D. turn yourself in: real Guys don't dye their hair blond

Fight Embellishment

Always embellish the retelling of the story about how you got your butt kicked in a fight. Cite numerous opponents, unfair advantages, or anything else that will support your case. You must weave your web of distortion to prove that no other man could have done any better in the same situation. A true pro can tell his story so well that he can proclaim that he got his butt kicked with pride.

SIDEBAR

Never tell a story that has possible embellishments of fact when a buddy who saw the fight is with you. If you need help with the story, your buddy will embellish for you. Either tell it like it is or let your buddy lead the way.

POP QUIZ

If you notice a Guy giving you signals that he's tired:

- **A.** make sure you tell him to keep working
- **B.** assure him that a break is coming
- **C.** treat him like trash for not keeping up
- **D.** that's an indication that it's okay to call it a day
- **E.** work another half hour

I Know I'm Really Fat When . . .

As the years go on, increase the level at which you determine yourself to be *too* fat. The holes in your belt, like rings on a tree, show especially good growth years. There is no set weight for when you're too fat. It's just graded on the curve.

POP QUIZ

How can you totally recover after a poor performance in sawing some wood?

- **A.** salvaging a bent nail
- **B.** buying the next round of beer
- **C.** making an entertaining excuse
- **D.** ripping on the previous home owner

Keeping Up with Your Buddy

When you're doing stuff with your buddy in his town, and it's something he enjoys or is good at, you have to pretend like you know what you're doing. Whether it's hiking up a hill, and you're so fat and out of breath that you think you might die, or rock climbing, and you're so scared of heights that you think you're definitely going to die, you must never reveal these true feelings. Besides, your buddy is doing all that to try to impress you anyway—it's not as if he goes hiking in the Grand Canyon every weekend. When you're with your buddy, in his town, be sure to keep up with him and look comfortable doing it.

SIDEBAR

Remember, be the survivor and not the hero—you have the entire day to prove your worth.

Official Introduction

It is vital to shake hands with another Guy during the "official introduction." It is okay to hold a conversation or even drink beer together before the exchange. After names have been exchanged, however, you must incorporate the handshake at that time. If a handshake is not reciprocated, you will open a rupture within the natural order of things, forcing an egotistical showdown of who's more unsociable.

SIDEBAR

No matter how slimy the other Guy's wet-noodle handshake may be, never crush his hand. Just hold the handshake a bit longer than he does, which will send the "confidence message."

Snake Bites

When you're hiking with your buddy in areas where poisonous snakes are found and you get bitten while "answering the call" behind some rock or bush, the GuyRule is that you're gonna die.

Speak Up

When you're in a classroom and you have something to say, speak up. The complexity of the question you ask will establish your place in the pecking order. Ask something that gives all the other Guys a good idea of your level of knowledge. Just don't be the Guy who incessantly asks off-task, irrelevant questions, annoying everybody.

By never saying anything in class, you send the weak message to all the other Guys that you're not confident enough in yourself to put your opinion on the line. Be a man and put yourself out there.

You must know the difference between "do it yourself" and:

- **A.** having it done right
- **B.** a hack job
- **C.** ruin it yourself
- **D.** doing it with a buddy

Swimming Pool Rules

At a swimming pool, Guys must at some point take their shirts off. There's a feeling of "shirt peer pressure" that compels every Guy there to risk his own fat exposure, rather than just assume the "fat Guy" role by leaving his shirt on. If there're women around when he takes his shirt off, he must pull the gut in and make it as taut as possible, while puffing his chest out.

SIDEBAR

The only thing worse than the fear of fat exposure is fat exposure coupled with the "terrible tan."

POP QUIZ

What isn't looked upon favorably by your buddies when swapping "most famous person I've met" stories?

A. when you make up parts of the encounter to spice it up

B. when you ramble on about it and it wasn't a big deal

C. if you were too awed by your sports hero to say anything to him

D. when it wasn't you who actually met the person but you know somebody who knows somebody . . .

The Leg Touch

When you are sitting next to another Guy and you encounter the "leg touch," it is imperative that you both make an adjustment to ensure that it doesn't happen again. There is a maximum of only two "accidental" leg incursions before one of the Guys starts to get nervous.

When a Guy gets out of the water, it is vital that he pull the bathing suit away from his now shrunken crotch unless:

- **A.** he doesn't care who sees him
- **B.** he has a huge penis
- **C.** his wife has seen it before
- **D.** he is going to get back in the water soon

You're *Never* Lost

Guys are *never* lost and they *never* need a map. They've just chosen to take an alternate route at this particular juncture.

SIDEBAR

If you are by yourself and you know that you are in fact lost, drive around only as long as you are not infringing on the start of an appointment. If you are getting dangerously close to being late for a meeting, stop for directions at a convenience store, purchase something, and then ask how to find the place. Never go into the store just to ask for directions.

Man and machine are most at one when moving less than five miles an hour, and nowhere is this more apparent than:

- **A.** when learning to drive a five-speed
- **B.** when hooking up a trailer
- **C.** in the display of their parking prowess
- **D.** backing up a trailer

Your Favorite Brand

Guys must be loyal to their product brand for things like trucks, beer, oil, women, and even batteries. Once a Guy's been using a brand of something for a while, he'll stick to it and swear by it. Even if he's actually sick of it and wants to try something different, he's talked about his brand to his buddies for so long that he simply cannot make the switch. He's stuck with it, because admitting that his brand is inferior would disturb the social equity that Guys try to maintain with one another.

SIDEBAR

 Some Guys will be able to point out every minute detail of the product. Even if they had to take their favorite brand of whatever back to the store fifty times to get it repaired under warranty, they will claim they never had a problem with it.

Chapter 4
Home Fires

GUY
HOME FIRES

Be it in the kitchen, the garage, or the store, we are all forced to cross the no-man's-land of the domestic battleground. Nowhere are there more opportunities to personalize your own protocol than in your home. A stack of remote controls may seem unnecessary to some, but to you they're your lifeline to the sporting world. Volume controls at a touch with precision tuning are what separates man from beast. An entertainment center is not a piece of furniture, it is a temple of worship, constructed for family and friends. It is the sacred battleground of many a war waged over control of your god box.

Every Guy has experienced the rigors of packing for a move, or traversed traffic for a midnight trip to the store. Every Guy can recite his story of a trip in a packed car that lasted too long. As you travel your way through this chapter, we ask you to remember that there is no better place to be than in your home, stoking those home fires. Be it with your wife or with a buddy, remember: Your home is your castle.

Yet there comes a time when you must leave your sanctum. Stepping out of the safe confines of your home brings with it a unique set of circumstances. This journey through the home fires of Guydom is one trip you are sure to enjoy.

Bachelor Dishes

Bachelors must be able to work in dirty dishes like da Vinci worked in oil. Never impose an artificial time frame on doing your dishes. Only wash your dishes when the smell is so bad that you can't stand it, your neighbors call the board of health on you, or you are completely out of dishes and you have already washed the same plate and fork five times.

SIDEBAR

It is possible that your guilt will get the best of you. You have been a very "clean" Guy in the past while living at your parents' home. It may in fact be that your mess is a direct result of having to learn a new schedule because you are too busy to do the dishes, or you are away from home for the first time and are living out some liberal protest against your parents' authority.

POP QUIZ

If your wife doesn't like you to party, what do you tell your partying friends?

A. Sorry, I can't party. You know . . . the wife thing.
B. She's cool with it.
C. I'll have a couple.
D. Oh, what the hell!
E. NULL

Checkout Lane Selection

No matter how tempted you may be, never play musical lanes while checking out at the store. Regardless of which lane you choose, it'll be the wrong one, so simply find the lane with the best-looking woman working the cash register, or standing in line. When it's time to pay, never write a check; it's strictly cash or credit. Just pick your lane and stick with it, because if you don't, when the Muzak stops, the checkout lane gauntlet will get the best of you.

SIDEBAR

Every Guy who goes to the store will make a mental tally of how much everything costs, rounding everything up to the nearest dollar just to ensure that they have enough money. By the time they check out, they will feel a sense of relief that they had enough money to pay for the stuff. No Guy should ever go back through the line to pick up an item they wanted but did not get because they thought they couldn't afford it. Get it next time.

Christen the Toilet

When helping a buddy move into a new place, it is not acceptable to sit down and use the toilet before your buddy has. The toilet is yet another tool to Guys. Don't use this tool before your buddy has had a chance to craft his own masterpiece. Destroying your buddy's toilet with the remnants of the greasy, on-the-move lunch is not acceptable.

SIDEBAR

You must refrain from nosing about the place until the new owner has had a chance to do so first. Running the water faucets, exploring rooms, and rifling through the cabinets before he does is way out of line.

POP QUIZ

If the driver has the vents pointed toward him, and he knows it, and he doesn't give it up:

A. you can reach over and move them yourself
B. yell at the Guy and ask him what he was thinking
C. think of ways to get him into your sweltering car
D. that's a "breach of the worst fashion"

Commitment to Making the Fire

The Guy who commits to starting the campfire must follow through, stopping at nothing short of napalm to start that fire.

SIDEBAR

 Wet-wood plausible deniability helps support your case for using gas or lighter fluid in extreme situations. Get the wife warm first, then reinstitute protocol.

SIDEBAR

Only resort to using gas or lighter fluid to start the fire if all other means have been exhausted. You absolutely cannot go right in there, pour fluid all over, and start the fire. If you disagree, just try it, then look to your buddies for approval. You'll find that you were sadly mistaken and won't live it down the whole camping trip.

POP QUIZ

Never eat the last piece of pizza because:

- **A.** respect for the kill is vital
- **B.** you never know when you will eat another piece
- **C.** you don't need it
- **D.** you need to save room for beer

Controlling Your Grill

You control your own domain of grilldom. No other Guy can come in there and fire up your grill. You own that grill. The difference between firing up a Guy's grill and making a pass at his wife is that you might live if you make a pass at his wife.

SIDEBAR

You throw a party at your place and all your buddies come over for burgers and brews. Everybody's hanging out, swapping embellishments, and you go out back to fire up your grill for the big burger rage. Your buddy Phil is standing there in front of your rig, fire blazing. "Oh hi," he says, "I fired up your grill for you. It's all ready to go!" Please. I don't think so.

POP QUIZ

If you're a passenger in your buddy's car and a good song comes on the radio, what do you do?

- **A.** reach over and turn it up, then explain later
- **B.** don't say anything, but hope your buddy turns it up
- **C.** ask your buddy to turn it up because the driver has exclusive rights to the radio
- **D.** do nothing

Drinking the Hard Stuff

When you're passin' around the hard liquor or the swill, no matter how hard it hits your gut, swallow it, and keep a stone face. Then wink and say, "Yeah, that was good booze." This is the grown-up version of eating worms or ingesting other things that make you want to vomit.

SIDEBAR

Everyone else is just praying that they can also withstand their drink. In this senseless way, all Guys inadvertently encourage each other, even though everyone there hates the taste of the liquor as it hits the gut wrong.

POP QUIZ

When you're playin' basketball, it's quite acceptable to:

- **A.** call a foul if you get burned on a play
- **B.** not call a foul on yourself if you can get away with it
- **C.** act as if somebody had just cut your nuts off when you get fouled
- **D.** use an old high school injury for plausible deniability

Fire Is Really Important to Guys

Fire was the start of GuyRules. It was one of the first really cool things that Guys had control over. Today, starting a fire is the return to primeval Guydom, even though the primeval urge to pull your woman into the tent by her hair has been lost.

SIDEBAR

 For the city dweller who has perfected his ability to select the right fake log and start it with only one match, there is no greater challenge than having to start a fire with last week's newspapers and small sticks.

POP QUIZ

When you're running late to the airport, you must:

- **A.** be willing to cut people off, if need be
- **B.** stay cool
- **C.** make the people in the car keep quiet while you drive
- **D.** blame your wife for taking too long

Grocery Cart Selection

At the grocery store, Guys must be able to select a properly working cart from the first three carts in the lineup. If you must use a cart, being able to find a good one quickly is an indispensable skill. Nothing is worse than banging and skidding your way through the "honey-do" list in the feminine-hygiene aisle when you are trying to be discreet.

SIDEBAR

 The natural tendency is for a basket, oddly enough. The basket is really the high-speed, low-drag, express-lane, cash-only move for a Guy with twelve items or less. But sometimes the cart is the only option. For example, when you are stocking up on dog chow or cases of beer for the upcoming project, you need a cart. Be sure that cart is up to snuff before entering the grocery store's highways and byways.

POP QUIZ

Especially when working together on a project, each Guy will have:

- **A.** his own set of sawhorses
- **B.** his own cooler, full of beer
- **C.** his own crazy theory on how to proceed
- **D.** his own hammer

Grocery Store Right-of-Way

Married Guys shopping for their wives have the right-of-way over both single Guys and couple-shoppers. They have the complete respect of all Guys at the grocery store because their "honey-do" list lies in the produce aisle or, worse yet, the "feminine hygiene" aisle. They blow right through three-way stops with single-Guy-shoppers and couple-shoppers to complete the mission, and return to the castle. The single-Guy-shopper (look for the canned pasta or frozen pizza to spot them) must yield at intersections to all others.

Initial Tent Setup

The only time you are allowed to use the directions for setting up your tent is when it is new. You must always memorize your initial tent setup. Once you have successfully set up your tent, you are compelled to discard the directions and the box the tent came in. If you can't set up your tent from memory, you should not be camping.

SIDEBAR

If you are less than confident in your understanding of how to set up your new tent, find a way to hold a conversation with a buddy so you can mask your incompetent mistakes behind "absentminded" chatter. Never set up your tent with your wife unless you have all the procedures down pat.

POP QUIZ

The Guy with the ugliest scar coupled with the most grotesque story will:

A. show it to his kids at every turn

B. pretend that it didn't hurt

C. make up some war-injury story to match

D. win the "scar-off" Olympics

Internal Surf Clock

Every Guy must develop his internal TV channel-surf clock. A true Guy will be able to surf as many channels as possible during any commercial, being able to check sports scores or make a complete trip around the dial without missing a single second of the show he was watching. The master of this art is the one who can flash back to his show while the screen is just fading into the program.

SIDEBAR

The protocol surrounding the TV remote control is abundant and cross-cultural. Check out how many rules have come in about it from all around the world at www.guyrules.com. [Remove shameless plug before publication.]

POP QUIZ

If you're the type of Guy who leaves tools and material lying all over the site until the end of the day, but your host is the type of Guy who picks things up along the way, you:

- **A.** stand by your habits
- **B.** drink more beer
- **C.** offer help, knowing he won't accept
- **D.** follow the host's lead

Knob Faux Pas

Man, like most animals, is territorial in nature. Nowhere is this more prevalent than in the Guy's home. It is a total breach of Guydom to start messing around with the stereo and TV in your buddy's place. This "knob faux pas" applies to the car as well. The general rule of thumb is Don't play with another Guy's knobs.

SIDEBAR

Hands off your buddy's stuff. Guys understand this creed except when they're drunk and proclaim themselves the new deejay of the party.

When you make eye contact with a woman in a club, you must do the following before bragging to the boys:

- **A.** verify that she's good looking
- **B.** establish a second confirmation contact
- **C.** pound your beer for all to see
- **D.** set up the scope for your buddies' approval

Mismatching the Plates

It is perfectly acceptable to mismatch kitchen plates when a buddy comes over for chow. In fact, when a Guy mismatches the plates, it makes the other Guy feel more at home. If he places matching plates in front of his buddy, it signals that he has been, at some time, under the spell of a woman.

SIDEBAR

The worst thing that can happen is to be under the spell of the one woman who represents the ultimate threat to Guydom: Mom.

POP QUIZ

If you grind a gear:

- **A.** push the clutch in again and shift
- **B.** blame it on the clutch
- **C.** act as if nothing happened
- **D.** fight the instinct to look around to see if anyone heard you

Packing Czar

In his home, every Guy must establish his dominance as the packing czar. Nowhere is this more important than in the preparation of the car for a road trip. As czar, the Guy must be willing to bark orders to his minions and have them bring items in sequence according to his packing schema. He must be able to pack insurmountable quantities of luggage into the trunk of his car with complicated precision, reminiscent of the moves used to solve the puzzle of the Rubik's Cube.

SIDEBAR

Trip preparation can include checking for the keys, changing the oil, checking tire pressure, checking for the wallet, buying and packing food, checking for the keys, loading the car, checking for the keys, and of course, making the final check: spectacles, testicles, wallet, and watch.

SIDEBAR

When the car's almost packed, be prepared because the wife will bring out the beach chairs and the unplanned second cooler.

Pet Talk

You cannot talk pet talk in front of your buddies. If you must address your pet in front of your friend, it's in formal tongue only. Under no circumstances may you pucker your face in some kind of kissing gesture toward your pet. You'll lose any respect from the Guys around you and set their homophobic defenses to *red alert.*

POP QUIZ

If you're working on a project, and your book editor gets laid off due to a new corporate outlook:

- **A.** see if you can shop your book somewhere else
- **B.** ask your agent just what is going on over there
- **C.** get a case of beer and work through it
- **D.** don't panic

The Garage Is Your Kingdom

Every Guy must establish control over his garage. If the house is his castle, then the garage is his bastion. If he loses control over other parts of his castle in a frontal family assault, he must defend his tool chest and workbench with flanking fire to the bitter end.

POP QUIZ

When is it okay to call pass interference when watching a football game?

- **A.** when you desperately hope that it really is
- **B.** only when you're willing to put your reputation on the line that it really is
- **C.** when the refs have been making bad calls all day
- **D.** when you know it isn't true, but are trying to cover your favorite receiver's butt
- **E.** when it means the game

Three Types of Campers

There are three types of campers. The first is the mister-let's-go-anywhere-that-this-four-wheel-drive-can-go-and-we'll-put-some-logs-together-for-a-shitter kind of camper. The second is the we've-gotta-go-where-there's-a-rest-room-get-a-camp-site-where-you-hang-a-ticket kind of camper. Finally, there's the full-blown self-contained-above-ground-moving camper-atus. Guydom dictates that you really can't say anything about the other Guy's form of camping, because you're just as adamant about your style as he is about his.

SIDEBAR

Every Guy must carry in his camperatus a collection of tools that he will need in order to set up and maintain his campsite. His collection of ropes, axes, saws, and rain gear must prepare him for almost any event short of a hurricane.

Washing Off the Plates

A Guy who's in tune with the ways of Guydom will always follow the host's lead when it comes to washing off the plates after eating at a buddy's house. If the host washes off his plate and puts it in the dishwasher, his buddy must follow suit. If, on the other hand, the host leaves his dishes where they'll sit until even the maggots look for a better place to live, it would be a tragic show of disrespect to clean up one's own dishes. This sends the condescending message that "Heh you're a scumbag and I lead a cleaner lifestyle."

SIDEBAR

Some Guys will use every last dish, some of them more than once, before washing any, or even buy new ones before submitting to the wretched chore.

Chapter 5

Hygiene

GUY HYGIENE

For years Guys have taken the high ground and proclaimed themselves exempt from criticism over their hygiene rituals. The time has come to set a few things straight. While no real Guy would ever claim allegiance to hair gel for too long, or admit to packing a hair dryer on a trip, there are strict regulations by which they operate.

Nowhere are these hygiene rules more evident than in expulsion of gas, the washing of clothes, or preparation for a date. While some of us guard these rituals like Pentagon secrets, others share them with anyone who will listen (or smell). It has been argued that it is hygiene that sets Guys apart from gals and that may be true, but it is also what bonds us together as Guys.

This chapter unlocks these closely guarded secrets. In short, it can be summed up in a few words: gas, grundies, guts, and girls.

Blonds

Real Guys don't dye their hair blond (for example: Dennis Rodman, David Bowie, George Michael).

 When you walk into your favorite deli and your old acquaintance behind the counter, Mr. Jet-Black Hair, smiles at you from beneath newly dyed blond hair, you're suddenly in a tough spot. Your instinct drives you to rib him about it, but you hesitate because clearly the Guy thinks he's slick, and you don't want to offend somebody you only know on a sandwich basis.

POP QUIZ

You're at the gas station filling up the cruiser. The pump stops at the desired amount but . . .

- **A.** you quickly remove the nozzle and replace it in the pump
- **B.** you pretend you are an adult film star, pull out the nozzle, and spray down the car
- **C.** do that shake-squeeze, handle-rattle-hose method to get the last little bit of gas
- **D.** real men don't have cars, they have Harleys
- **E.** you let your wife/girlfriend pump the gas for you, while you go in and pay for it

Brief Elasticity

As a bachelor, you must maintain strict standards for the longevity of your underwear. As long as the elastic is tight around your waist, then under no circumstances should you ever feel compelled to discard your grundies. Despite the skids marks, and even if the muffler is rusted out, they are still serviceable.

POP QUIZ

While at the movies, and sitting next to some other Guy:

- **A.** be happy if the Guy doesn't talk to you
- **B.** ask him questions and talk to him constantly
- **C.** lose some battles, but win the war
- **D.** offer him popcorn

Cleanest Pair of Dirty Clothes

As a bachelor, there comes a point in time during the week when you have to find your cleanest pair of dirty clothes. Each major piece of clothing must pass the "sniff test" before being worn for yet another day. Wait until *after* you've showered before making your decision.

SIDEBAR

When you find yourself without clean clothes, you must have an order of cleanliness. You can wear a pair of pants longer than a pair of socks, a dress shirt longer than a T-shirt, and sweatshirts longer than dress shirts. However, never subject yourself to the "sniff test" on socks. Assume that dirty socks stink.

POP QUIZ

The "fat-Guy" rule states that you're supposed to, as the years go on:

- **A.** pull your shirt out so you can hide your gut
- **B.** blame your wife's cooking for making you fat
- **C.** tell your friends that your fat gut is "bought and paid for"
- **D.** increase the level at which you consider yourself to be *too* fat

Cologne Signification

Cologne signifies that you're on an official date. Not just any date, but the kind when you've gotta slap on *the* cologne. You've gotta wear your most expensive, very special stuff. You may be going to the same exact place where you always go, except that you're wearing *the* cologne.

SIDEBAR

If you bump into your buddies on the way out to the date, they might give you a little trouble over the "perfume," but deep down they envy the fact that you might score tonight.

POP QUIZ

When you step up to the tee, start making excuses before you even hit your first shot:

- **A.** so you can feel better about your slice
- **B.** so the other Guys will back off their game
- **C.** to establish plausible deniability
- **D.** so you have time to warm up
- **E.** so you can overcome the first-hole jitters

Grading Farts

It's imperative that when the Guy next to you farts you make an effort to give it a grade. And you have to be fair, even if you don't like the Guy.

You have to be fair with your assessment. Criteria include volume, stink, and duration. When it's really bad, you have to offer token resistance to the fart, but in reality you have profound respect for the Guy who just blew you away.

POP QUIZ

Being outwardly comfortable with a big, stinky weed hanging out of your face is:

- **A.** pure Guydom
- **B.** a sign of a man
- **C.** not the best thing to attract chicks
- **D.** downright stupid

Hair Dryer

Never spend too much time in front of a hair dryer. Every Guy has occasionally needed a little help with the rug, but don't stand in front of the mirror and pretend that you're some Hollywood stud-muffin. If you need to blow-dry your hair, blow-dry your hair, but don't forget you're still a Guy.

SIDEBAR

 If you find yourself standing in front of the mirror, wishing you had a defuser and contemplating up-grading your hair dryer, you had better rethink your hair style.

POP QUIZ

When at the grocery store and you need a cart for the weekly catch:

A. pick one that has a baby seat. It's a great way to meet women by asking if they've seen your three-year-old nephew

B. real Guys just try to carry everything they need without using a cart

C. pick a worthy steed to carry the weekly bounty

D. the wife does the shopping cause you can't handle money responsibly

Matching Clothes

Never leave the house without deferring to your wife or girl-friend for clearance on the matching of clothes. Even though you've been dressing yourself all this time, you have to act as if you don't know if the tie and shirt are really going to work. You'll score some points for consulting her superior wisdom, and you won't go to work looking like your dad.

SIDEBAR

It's really not worth fighting her on an outfit that you think matches perfectly. She can see subtle shades and patterns that are beyond your more crude perceptive capabilities. Give in to her, change your shirt, and save the card for some other situation that's on more even ground.

POP QUIZ

Short of grinding your gears, there is no worse automotive offense than:

    A. starting your already-running car
    B. hitting the curb while parallel parking
    C. hitting the curb while making a U-turn
    D. bumping the car in front of you while parking

Musty Shirts

When a bachelor leaves clothes in the washer too long, and his shirts develop a musty smell, it's acceptable to wear them if he slaps on enough cologne. However, he cannot wear a rotting shirt when he's going out on a first date. If he is in danger of detection, he must get a completely different shirt, even if he has to borrow one from a buddy.

SIDEBAR

There are few things worse than having to borrow a shirt from your buddy. Few Guys can handle the smell of another Guy's stinky pits embedded in his shirt. Only borrow your buddy's clothes as a last, desperate resort.

POP QUIZ

When you have the perfect get-rich scheme:

- **A.** tell everybody about it
- **B.** get your wife's approval on it
- **C.** do lots of research to validate the idea
- **D.** tell only a select few, those buds you can trust
- **E.** quit your job and go for it

Sharing the Fart

This seemingly complex ritual, "to fart or not to fart," can be mastered. A Guy can't fart too soon with a new buddy. If he's in his buddy's car or home, it's acceptable to fart *only* after his buddy has farted. Farting terms for Guys are just as important as butt-sniffing terms are for dogs. It's the way Guys share what's really inside them.

SIDEBAR

You can't fart too soon unless you feel comfortable chancing a quick, low-pressure release while your buddy is out of the room.

When your buddy gets a new vehicle:

A. you should ask to go for a ride
B. pretend that you don't care
C. it is required that you say something nice about it
D. point out your vehicle

Ultimate Burp

One of the true measures of Guydom is how well a Guy can burp. There's always the spontaneous rattle-in-the-throat, almost-hurts-your-neck kinda burp. Then there's the I've-never-really-expected-that-burp-after-I've-eaten-jalapeños-blow-it-in-the-other-guy's-face burp. The lowest echelon of burp is performed by the Guy who sucks air into his gut and spells words like "bullshit" with the burp.

SIDEBAR

 Among Guys the belch is a true work of art, expressed by each in his own unique way. Compliments must be swapped, as well as comments describing the character of the belch. It's rumored that the stomach acid in a Guy's stomach after a night of drinking can eat straight through a mahogany bar.

POP QUIZ

Guys are more stubborn than stupid, so to show what they can do, they must:

- **A.** do it themselves
- **B.** be willing to bark orders
- **C.** never make excuses
- **D.** have your kids watch you work
- **E.** explain everything like you're giving a university lecture

Washing Your Hands in the Men's Room

When in a public rest room with at least one other Guy, be sure to wash your hands. When another Guy is around, the hand-washing ritual should become even more vigorous, with the use hot water, extra soap, and hand scrubbing. You never know—he might be on the job-interview team that you're about to sit before.

SIDEBAR

 It is quite acceptable to hold a conversation with a Guy while washing hands. Never spend too much time jawing with another Guy, however—get in and get out.

POP QUIZ

After striking out in baseball never:

A. blame the umpire to hide your failure
B. look at the bat as if it could yield a reason for your blunder
C. kick dirt at the catcher
D. talk trash to the pitcher

Chapter 6
Party

GUY PARTY

Every Guy parties to some extent. The party event and activities are vital to the very survival of a well-balanced Guy. What constitutes this activity varies greatly from one Guy to the next, but the concept and need remains the same. To party is to either celebrate achievement, relieve the mundane, or escape the ugly.

From hitting the bars every night to just having one drink, a pipe, or a cigar before bed, we all have our own version of the lighter side of life. The continuous challenge is to remain in control of your partying, or at least to give the appearance that you are, if you insist on kidding yourself.

Of course, it is dangerous to howl at the moon too often, as we all have experienced at some time. You come home two hours late from the bar and your wife makes sure it's clear to you just how stupid you are. You find that you're spending too much cash at happy hour with all the other people from work who are desperate for any excuse to go out and forget about the grind for a while. You find that you just can't redefine yet again how fat you think you are, as you can no longer fit into your pants.

You must temper your impulses with a bit of wisdom and restraint to successfully glide through the waters of moderation. At least, that's what the theory is, though it hasn't yet been demonstrated to our knowledge.

Backsplash

If you're drinking out of the same beer bottle with a buddy, don't allow any backwash to slip into the bottle. Bring the bottle down slightly so the pressure is released off the top lip. You must avoid a hostile beer takeover at all costs. Share the beer, not your bodily fluids.

SIDEBAR

The exception to this is when a Guy chooses to force a "beer takeover" by purposefully causing massive backsplash, so that the other Guy won't take it back. This is only done among good buddies who make a habit of pissing each other off.

POP QUIZ

A true pro can tell his story about a fight so well that he can proclaim:

- **A** that he won the fight
- **B.** that he got his butt kicked with pride
- **C.** that he didn't need any help from his buddies
- **D.** that the other Guy was crying when he got done with him

Crushing of the Can

If your buddies are coming over to help on a project, you don't offer beer in bottles. You offer it in a can. This allows for displays of testosterone in which they crush and throw the can when they've finished their beer. Most important, when a Guy opens a can, he knows that he's in Guydom. That primeval *pwhoosh* sound is a signal to all Guys: This is where they belong.

SIDEBAR

Nothing is more satisfying than crushing a can after a hard day of work on a project. Often, Guys will compete with different techniques, and compare the resulting disks of aluminum for style points to determine who gets the last beer.

POP QUIZ

When you're working with a buddy and it comes to the point when you know he screwed up, and he knows he screwed up, you must:

- **A.** laugh at him, give him a beer, and take over
- **B.** give him an out
- **C.** thoroughly explain in great detail your plan about how to salvage the project
- **D.** challenge him to a grill-out to determine his fate
- **E.** tell all your other buddies about it repeatedly

Don't Eat the Last Piece

Since the Stone Age, respect for the kill has always been important to Guys. Never eat the last piece of pizza.

SIDEBAR

No matter how much pizza there is, everyone will just attack it and ravenously eat the whole thing, except for that one last piece that everyone covets but nobody touches.

POP QUIZ

Finishing first is a bonus, but:

A. the first Guy done has to buy the first round of drinks

B. only if the quality is there

C. only if you're paid enough

D. don't forget to hide your mistakes behind paint

Get One for Everyone

When heading to the fridge to grab a beer, by god, get one for everyone. A Guy is compelled to offer a beer to every Guy there. The protocol changes depending on how well he knows each Guy. There's the "hey-welcome-to-the-club" grab you a beer, ending with the old "point-wink-gotcha-on-the-list-already" grab you a beer. If your buddies are working outside and it's hot and you don't get one for everyone, that's the queen mother of all breaches of beer etiquette.

SIDEBAR

 There is no better feeling than walking into a room and having a buddy hand you an ice-cold beer without having to ask for it. Guys have gone to war over the loyalty gained by such gestures of Guydom.

Making the Break

When at a party and the pleasantries have been exchanged with other couples, Guys must skillfully employ the art of ditching their wives. The real party doesn't start until all the Guys are out back together, hanging around the grill, drinking beers and swapping stories. By waiting for the moment when the wife is engaged in conversation, the Guy can create the impression that the slip was instituted by her.

SIDEBAR

If there is a Guy who is not tied down with a woman, he must instigate the first-stage separation so other Guys can follow suit. A Guy who is "hard at work" on the grill must request assistance from his buddies so they can make their break. Plausible deniability is a beautiful thing.

Sweaty Alien Costume

Don't razz the Guy who shows up at a Halloween party sweating profusely in some rubber-masked alien costume. Guys are self-conscious enough when it comes to dressing out of the norm, so don't ridicule him. At least he showed up in costume. It is, however, okay to laugh with him when he lifts up his mask, in an effort to commiserate. Besides, that phaser he's sporting might be a real one, after all.

SIDEBAR

The Guy probably went back and forth about whether or not he should go through with wearing the costume. He committed to it, so he has to see it through all the challenges, which include eating and drinking with the mask on, breathing through the suffocating mask, and ignoring the rivers of sweat running down his neck and back.

Teeth and Beer

Every Guy must be a virtual MacGuyver of beer-bottle opening. When faced with opening a bottle with no twist-off cap
(real beer), and there's no tool at hand, always improvise.
Every Guy will find a way to open the beer, using whatever is
at hand. Score extra points for using organic objects like a
rock or stick. Only in final desperation can you attempt to
open a beer with your teeth.

Younger Guys may want to live up to the fraternity-
house myth by trying to pop the top off a beer bottle
with their teeth. You don't see Guys at parties trying
to tighten a bolt with their molars. Same concept.

**You're compelled to call out when you feel your team
should take a time-out, but always avoid:**

- **A.** blowing your cool and calling it at the wrong time
- **B.** whining about not having any time-outs left
- **C.** screaming for the time-out before the play is over
- **D.** blaming the coach because he's just having
  an off night
- **E.** making unqualified judgments about the coach

That First Beer

When you're working on a project with a Guy, it's important to know when to offer that first beer. Most people say noon, but that's just a guideline. Just slip the beer offer in with a list of other things people think are normal to drink at 10:30 in the morning. Something like "Hey, did I forget to offer you something? I can get you some coffee, cola, ice tea, beer . . ."

SIDEBAR

Every Guy will be wondering when it is appropriate to start drinking. Generally, the Guy that drinks on a daily basis will "kick off" the event by suggesting the first beer. You can always play the "reluctant virgin" even if you really want to start drinking yourself.

POP QUIZ

If a Guy's buddies are coming over to help on a project, it is completely inappropriate to offer beer in glass bottles because:

- **A.** cans are a lot cheaper
- **B.** canned beer gets warm too soon
- **C.** girls drink out of bottles
- **D.** you destroy the satisfaction gained by the sound of opening the can
- **E.** you can put more cans into the fridge

The Big Switch

Guys always stick with their staple beer. They are compelled to stick with it. When, in the midst of the project, it's come to the dreaded moment of switching beer brands, don't fear change. At least there is still beer left.

SIDEBAR

There's something inherent to Guys that dictates that you've got to drink, and continue to drink, the same exact beer you start with. No matter what, you must stick with that sucker all night long. If you start on one beer, you are stuck with it, even if, given the chance to start over, you would have chosen another brand. That's the beer you're drinking that night; live with it.

POP QUIZ

When the Guy next to you farts, you must:

- **A.** be unfair about the grade you give it because you don't like the Guy
- **B.** act like you didn't hear it
- **C.** attempt to give it a fair grade, even if you don't like the Guy
- **D.** take credit for it
- **E.** act as if you're appalled

The Trump Goes Bad

When you're trying to trump another Guy's bullshit and it turns out that he is actually right, his bullshit stands and he earns the right to "slam you home," either now or later. But rest assured, it is coming.

 If your buddy makes the "trump attempt" and you know that what you are saying is totally correct, let him dig his own grave by allowing him to talk as long and as loud as possible. However, once you counter with the corroborating evidence, hold on to that card and slam it home once you get the chance. Remember, you earned that card, so let him sweat a little bit and pick the perfect time to institute the slam.

POP QUIZ

When a Guy throws something to you exceptionally well you must:

    A. ignore it, pretending it was no big deal

    B. whip around and throw it back to him as hard as you can

    C. acknowledge the good toss

    D. give him a difficult throw to catch in return, to test his mettle

Trumping the Bullshit

When a Guy realizes another Guy is talking a bunch of crap, it's acceptable to break in and call him on his bullshit. Trumping a Guy's bullshit is not only acceptable, but expected practice between Guys.

SIDEBAR

Don't go overboard. You must allow your buddy a healthy BS buffer. Calling him on everything would be denying him his right to exaggerate, and you'd be stripping him of his only protection from his own inadequacies.

POP QUIZ

The hand-washing ritual will become more vigorous for:

  A. the other Guy's benefit
  B. you when you have grease on your hands
  C. anyone who goes into a public rest room
  D. a Guy who is on a date

Chapter 7

Projects

GUY PROJECTS

In the beginning, we lived in cold, dark caves. Life was a series of reactions to the demands of survival. After a long time, we emerged at the top of the food chain, thanks to fire, tools, and dumb luck. It was at this point in man's development that the concept of the project evolved. Ancient examples of projects include the construction of simple shelters and weapons, as well as organizing hunts and ceremonies.

As Guys have evolved, the complexity and scope of projects has grown. Cities were built, wars were waged. Organized projects involving the great minds of countless Guys have resulted in forests of backyard decks, millions of fenceposts, rebuilt engines, and enough beer to fill the Atlantic Ocean thirty-seven times.

Natural systems of protocol have been developed that help to maintain order and increase productivity throughout a project. Who calls breaks? What percentage of time is spent talking about how to do the job, compared to actually doing it? We all know the words that are banned on a project site, how long to work a project, and how to show off that project to as many people as possible. Don't forget the pitfalls of working a project with your wife, as well as the technique used to make yourself feel better about your failed project.

Degrees of Vulgarity

Vulgarity is inversely proportional to the number of females present. In the postfeminist, politically correct corporate office, nary a "shit" is heard. On a construction site, "fuck" flies like a junebug in a hurricane. (Note: None of this applies to truck stops.)

SIDEBAR

A Guy who can weave his web of vulgarity on the job site and not seem disgusting is a rare breed indeed. When you are in mixed company, be sure to make no more than one "slip up," before catching yourself and switching to "choir boy" mode.

POP QUIZ

The only time you are allowed to use the directions for setting up your tent is:

- **A.** if you forgot how to set it up
- **B.** if you are not very smart
- **C.** when it is new
- **D.** if it is a complicated tent to set up

Editor Gets the Axe

If you're working on a project, and your book editor gets laid off due to a new corporate outlook, don't panic. You can't let them see you sweat. Senior editors, who will be picking up the pieces after the restructuring, can smell fear right over the phone. Just relax, act cool, and try to make small talk about the vicious corporate world.

SIDEBAR

While an editor is an important part of the writing process, he or she is not the most important. Remember, you can't sell what is not on the shelf. Get it written and then ship it off—you do have a signed contract, after all.

POP QUIZ

Only wash your dishes when the smell is so bad you can't stand it, or:

- **A.** you can't find anything to eat on
- **B.** make up an excuse to mask your mess
- **C.** you can't find any counter space
- **D.** the neighbors call the board of health

Half Your Time

Guys must try to prove their point through some twisted parody of logic. Especially when working together on a project, each Guy will have his own crazy theory about how to proceed. These debates consume half of the time, or more, depending on how intoxicated they are. No one has any idea what the hell the other Guys are talking about. In the end, the most stubborn Guy wins.

SIDEBAR

 No matter how lost you get in the explanation of your theory, try and stick to your discombobulated thought until you are able to make a full recovery and make at least some sense in what you are saying. This will allow for a little wiggle room so you can effectively use the old "See, that is exactly what I was saying" ploy.

POP QUIZ

Avoid at all costs entering into a repair project with:

- **A.** your mother-in-law
- **B.** your father-in-law
- **C.** your wife
- **D.** your brother-in-law

Hasty Quality?

Finishing first is a bonus, but only if the quality is there. There's always a nail-slinging-just-get-it-done Guy around, but you can't rush the quality Guy, and there's no slower animal than a man obsessed with quality.

SIDEBAR

 Both quality Guy and "hasty boy" are equally proud of their projects, one for the sake of its quality, the other for the sake of just how fast he accomplished it. It's up to the ever-honest buddies to lay down the final judgment on the project. They'll let you know where that fine line is between haste and waste.

It is quite acceptable to make eye contact with another Guy during a good-bye:

  A. true
  B. false

Know When to Call the Expert

You must know the difference between "do it yourself" and "ruin it yourself." Don't force the professional to diagnose and repair your attempted fix; realize when it's time to call in the expert. Better men than you have turned a twenty-minute job into a three-day affair. While you must attempt the repair yourself, don't be too proud to say "Uncle."

SIDEBAR

A full-scale attack on a project is a very respected thing in the war of home ownership. So too is a sound checkbook.

POP QUIZ

When in the midst of a project and it's come to the dreaded moment of switching beer brands:

- **A.** decide beforehand your next brand
- **B.** drink whatever your buddy is drinking
- **C.** ask what is available
- **D.** don't fear change

Let's Call It a Day

You don't want to be the first to call it a day when you're working with your buddies. If you notice a Guy giving you signals that he's tired, that's an indication that it's okay to say "Heh, let's call it a day." Choose wisely, because if you quit the project too soon, the other Guys will think you're lazy. It's a very tricky thing to call it a day.

SIDEBAR

 A true pro will be able to scope out the scene for the most opportune time to end the day's work. Old-timers will congregate around the water jug, have conversations about the progress of the work for the day, make an assessment, and then place a time frame on when everyone will quit working. This will normally occur on the half hour. No one ever quits a job at 5:19 or 6:27.

POP QUIZ

At the end of the night, don't forget to check:

- **A.** that you have money to get home
- **B.** you have your keys
- **C.** you can at least drive
- **D.** your early rejects

Lumber Selection

Guys secretly rate one another in their ability to select lumber that's appropriate for the project. Only your closest buddies can point out errors in the selection process. Others reserve the poor-lumber-selection excuse to use as plausible deniability later in the project to cover up their own mistakes.

SIDEBAR

If you're the home owner, the master of the project, and it's time to get some more lumber, bring a couple of buddies along to help you out. But here's the deal: You must do your best in selecting good lumber, and in return, they follow protocol by not jumping in and critiquing your selection. You must avoid warping and excessive knots and they must keep quiet and trust your judgment.

POP QUIZ

When hanging out with a buddy at your place, you must be willing to help him leave, so he can:

- **A.** come over and play some other night
- **B.** blame any tardiness on you
- **C.** say that it was you that kept him
- **D.** pretend that the time just slipped away

Mimic When Unsure

When a Guy is doing something with his buddy that takes a particular skill, and that Guy doesn't know what the hell he's doing, he never reveals this. He just stays cool, waiting until he gets an opportunity to watch and emulate. A clear sign of the "mimic when unsure" ploy is the equipment check or the tool-belt adjustment. Though aware of this ploy, his buddy must never lay his bullshit bare by letting the Guy know he's busted.

SIDEBAR

Even though the mimic-when-unsure ploy never really works, protocol must be followed. Any astute Guy will observe that his buddy hasn't started working yet because he's waiting for the chance to observe what must be done, then do it. No questions should be asked. If he goes through the proper adjustments, fiddling with his tape measure while making small talk, for example, or pretending like he's just kicking back for a bit before starting, then you are compelled to allow him the "covert" observation of the task you're performing. Don't bust him, it's just not worth throwing the project into chaos.

Project Critique

When you're walking down the street with your wife or girl-friend, and you notice somebody else's construction project, you must always comment on it, as if you know more about it than you really do. Go ahead, score some intellect points and impress the old lady. But when you're with your buddies, and one of them really knows what the hell he's talking about, don't blow your own cool by making a stupid comment.

SIDEBAR

Brag and ridicule cautiously. No ego slam is tougher to work yourself out of than when you're really playing up what a poor job some Guy did, and one of your buddies can't help but answer with, "Actually, that's the finest example of the Schmuckitelli splinking technique I've ever seen," and explains in front of everybody exactly why you were dead wrong.

SIDEBAR

If you are going to participate in the gladiator sport of project critique, be sure to come equipped with the experience and knowledge with which to compete. Be sure to know a lot about the project that you are talking about. There is nothing worse than being busted in a web of double talk. If you decide to give a dissertation about how something was built, your woman may get the idea and ask you to reproduce the project in question. If that happens, the old lady will bust you for sure.

Project Goes Bad

When a project goes bad, every Guy must stop and discuss at length who and what went wrong. Typically this takes twice as long as fixing the mistake would. There's always one Guy who suddenly becomes busy cleaning up the site, as if to cover for his poor project performance.

SIDEBAR

> The depth of the discussion can include diagrams, graphs, pencil-marked drawings, and, in some cases, vulgarity. Under no circumstances can discussions of another Guy's family or mother enter into the conversation.

POP QUIZ

If your wife stops you from leaving the house because your clothes don't match:

- **A.** act as if you don't know what matches or not
- **B.** bow your head in disgrace and skulk back to the bedroom
- **C.** tell her that you're ugly too but she married you anyway
- **D.** thank her for the compliment

Project with Your Wife

Avoid at all costs entering into a repair project with your wife. There is nothing worse than having to explain to her every aspect of the project and every unaccounted-for spare part left over, as if it were a home-repair show. Even worse, she will be privy to every stupid diagnostic that you make before you successfully fumble your way through completing the job.

SIDEBAR

Every Guy must be allowed to take as much time as he needs to repair a problem he has never seen before. It is great to be the magic man and simply walk into the room and state that you have the problem fixed. There is, however, nothing worse than having to explain every single screw-up. Work on the problem by yourself, and see if you can convince your wife to get you a cold one, kick back, and let you handle it.

POP QUIZ

If you find yourself in a "driving situation" in which you know you just barely escaped an accident, you must hope to:

A. keep your wife from yelling at you

B. keep from getting killed

C. find some wildlife around you can blame

D. be able to blame the other Guy

Showing Off the Project

Every time you finish a large home-improvement project, it's imperative that you drag every single human being you know through the gory project details. If you don't get enough visitors to satisfy this primeval urge, tell everybody at work about it. Maybe you'll coerce one of them into coming over to check it out.

SIDEBAR

 While every Guy has his personal plan for a backyard or interior home-improvement project, it is not until he has completed one that he can give the insider-trading details about how the whole project was done. Be sure to end every comment with how hard or how easy it is to do this or that.

POP QUIZ

Vulgarity is inversely proportional to:

A. the number of years you were in the service
B. the quantity of beers you consumed
C. the number of Guys present
D. the number of females present

Taking Breaks

Having earned his tenure as "Gray Back," the oldest Guy calls the breaks. He may be able to work harder and longer than the younger Guys, but that doesn't matter. The younger Guys can't call the breaks because they feel they must out-work the older Guy. They'll work themselves into the ground to avoid being shown up by the "Gray Back."

SIDEBAR

There are a couple of types of gray backs that you have to watch out for. The first is the Guy whose stubborn pride puts him on the fast track to a heart attack. It's almost impossible, but for his own good call the breaks yourself and make him take them along with everybody else. The other gray back that you should look out for is the Guy who at seventy still has a constitution that puts you and your thirty-some-thing buddies to shame. He'll never call the break, just to make you weak punks suffer.

POP QUIZ

When a Guy on the project has a pair of time-worn work gloves:

- **A.** you ridicule him for needing gloves
- **B.** you boast about taking it like a man, you never wear gloves
- **C.** you ask him to borrow his gloves when you need them
- **D.** you are compelled to pay respect to the Guy

Two Types of Building Guys

When the two different types of building Guys are working together, it's clearly the style of the host that takes precedence. There's Mr. Drop-It-as-you-use-it and Mr. Peg-Board-tool-outline. If you make a mess of Mr. Peg-Board's stuff, you're asking for a hissy fit. If you clean up after Mr. Drop It, you're throwing the delicate balance of Guydom into chaos.

SIDEBAR

 The downside to Mr. Peg-Board's technique is that he generally annoys the hell out of everybody else.

SIDEBAR

 The drawback to Mr. Drop It's style is that by the end of the day, when you're ready to relax, you have an hour of clean-up to do first. This is typically handled by simply ignoring it.

POP QUIZ

When stuck in traffic:

- **A.** stick to one lane after a maximum of three lane changes
- **B.** freak out and honk your horn
- **C.** check out the other cattle around you
- **D.** watch for flirt possibilities

Words That Are Banned on the Project Site

Every Guy knows in his heart the complete set of words that are absolutely banned from the project site or other all-Guy activities. Examples include "love," "nurture," "tender," "sensitive," "cute," "warm," "splendid," "pizzazz," and "fabulous." The list gets even longer when beer and cigars are involved.

SIDEBAR

When working with the boys, it is not only acceptable to talk about deep subjects, but it is a good thing as long as the conversation only lasts a short time. Topics can only include such deeply held convictions as the depth of the Green Bay Packers' secondary, how long it will be before the Cubs make it to the World Series, or if we will ever have instant replay in professional football.

POP QUIZ

When you're working on a project with a group of Guys, when do you offer that first beer?

- **A.** any time you damn well feel like it
- **B.** never before noon
- **C.** the moment your buddies come over, no matter what time it is
- **D.** offer it with a list of other things people think are normal to drink at 10:30 in the morning

Working Longer

When Guys are working on a project, there's always the one rookie Guy who wants to be the hero. Veteran Guys will use the standard "work ploy," in which they initially work hard enough to trick the rookie into working himself out. That's where they ease off a bit to achieve the ultimate show of Guydom: working longer. Be the survivor, complete the project.

POP QUIZ

A Guy puts up with guilt only as long as:

    A. it provides you with a tactical trump card
    B. there is a possibility of getting some later
    C. he can stand it
    D. his buddy is getting more guilt than he is

GUY RULES

Chapter 8
Sports

GUY SPORTS

We feel that there are far too many sports analogies to describe our everyday life, as well as millionaires selling soft drinks, so we have decided to forgo any hero worship here and instead concentrate on "Joe Lunch Pail."

You will not find a single athlete who wears the title of "hero" quoted anywhere in this book. This is a place for the real athlete, from the hacker to the professional TV referee, whose only prerequisite is to be a Guy.

We have no intention of waiting until the fourth quarter to make our full-court press. No way—we are here to point out the joys of sports through vicarious viewing or amateur replication. This is as it should be within the true nature of things.

Caution: Pass Interference

Be cautious when making a pass interference call too early in a play. Every Guy hates a buddy who yells out "Pass interference" in a weak moment of hope. Make the call only when you believe it to be pass interference, based upon your professional TV viewing knowledge. Never make a pass interference call hoping for a generous call on the part of the ref.

SIDEBAR

Don't be the Guy who calls everything, regardless of whether or not there's the slightest possibility that it's true. Everybody hates that Guy. He's not doing his team justice.

When is it acceptable to use the new toilet in your buddy's new place when you're helping him move in?

    A. only in extreme emergencies
    B. at just the right time
    C. after he has had a chance to craft his own masterpiece

Commentary Time-Out

Every Guy must think *he* alone knows when best to call a time-out while watching a football game. However, he must avoid screaming the call out before the play is over. Of course, he can criticize the slow reaction time of the highly paid coach if his team is losing.

SIDEBAR

It's perfectly acceptable to rant and rave at the TV set when you can see that a player is calling for a time-out and nobody else, including the ref, has seen it yet. Feel free to blame the officials if your team loses, because they didn't allow the time-out soon enough.

POP QUIZ

Should you validate a Guy's new terminology when he's sharing it with you?

- **A.** yes, give him the appropriate ooohs and aaahs
- **B.** yes, tell him how much you respect his smarts
- **C.** no, pretend like you know it all already
- **D.** no, tell him if he wants a pat on the back to go tell his wife

Exaggerated Foul

When you're playin' basketball, it's quite acceptable when you get fouled to roll around on the ground, acting for the first few seconds as if somebody has just cut your nuts off, then jump up and play ball like nothing ever happened. However, avoid this at all costs while playing football, because then you're considered a wuss.

SIDEBAR

This technique has been used so much that it's now a part of the protocol of the game. To get any play at all with the refs you have to make a really big deal out of a foul. If a Guy bumps you, jump back a yard and slide backward across the court, spinning if you can at all manage it. Otherwise, the call will go to the Guy who bumped you, who is at this point nursing his wrist in an attempt to play the victim.

POP QUIZ

Every Guy must establish control over:

- **A.** his boss
- **B.** his wife
- **C.** his garage
- **D.** his lawn mower

Going Deep

When you're warming up for a football game with your buddies and one of them takes off and goes deep, you are compelled to throw to that Guy, simply because he went deep. Otherwise, you transform him from hero to zero, and he *is* coming back to the huddle.

SIDEBAR

"Go deep, go deep . . . NOT!" Don't do it. Now your buddy's winded, spent for a few minutes, sucking air, and for what? So you could look like the master in control of his fate? Be the tougher Guy and actually risk showing everybody how well you can throw deep.

POP QUIZ

When at the swimming pool, there's a feeling of "shirt peer pressure" that compels every Guy to:

- **A.** suck his gut in
- **B.** complain that he has sensitive skin
- **C.** make excuses about why he needs to, before taking his shirt off
- **D.** risk his own fat exposure

Hitting the Bottoms of Your Cleats

Baseball is about looking cool. When stepping up to bat, it is imperative that you hit the bottom of your cleats, regardless of whether or not you have mud in them. For added effect, use a couple of bat weights while warming up.

SIDEBAR

Every player must have their own warm-up ritual. Hitting the bottom of your cleats is one of the most respected of these. Grabbing your crotch is a bit risqué, but is needed from time to time.

POP QUIZ

Every Guy must be a virtual MacGuyver of:

   A. worthless facts

   B. the use of bungee cords

   C. beer-bottle opening

   D. the collection of beer money on Friday night

New Gear Expectations

When on the court or field, never brag excessively to another Guy about your new gear before you have had a chance to use it. Every Guy must avoid the self-imposed pressure of his new purchase. You can always hope that new gear will tip the scales and allow you to triumph over your buddy, but always mask your purchase with silence. The new gear alone will be intimidation enough.

SIDEBAR

One Christmas, G got new racquetball gear. The works: new racket, eye protection, and shoes. He kept warning everybody about how he was going to kick butt with his new gear. Finally, he got his chance to play with his new gear. Shortly afterward, he went home and wrote this GuyRule.

POP QUIZ

What helps establish you in the classroom pecking order?

- **A.** how you dress
- **B.** acting cool and never saying a word
- **C.** the complexity of the questions you ask
- **D.** how much brain housing you have compared to the other Guys
- **E.** where you position yourself on the seating chart

Nice Hit!

When watching football, you are compelled to acknowledge the "good hit." The bone-crushing, helmet-cracking hit that even gets a "Boom" from John Madden must be acknowledged. It is irrelevant what team the player is on. If the player that gets hit plays for your buddy's team, you can rub it in, but not too much, because your Guy could be next.

SIDEBAR

Acknowledging the good hit always involves the "I can feel your pain" facial expression, accompanied by the quick sucking intake of air, followed by "Ooooh, that's gotta hurt." If the player gets right back up, everyone watching will give him credit for how tough he is, with fans of the opposing team doing this as quietly as possible while still fulfilling their duty.

POP QUIZ

What Guy possession are you expressly forbidden to borrow?

- **A.** his car
- **B.** his wife
- **C.** his clothes
- **D.** his tape measure
- **E.** his remote control

Pass Reception Critique

A true football fan must be willing to put his professional TV viewing reputation on the line by categorically making a call on a pass reception. You have to take a stand before the instant replay confirms or disproves your call. Only make a call if you are convinced beyond a shadow of a doubt that you're right. Your reputation in making pass reception calls is on the line, so don't foolishly risk it on a hasty call.

SIDEBAR

Was it a good catch or not? It's the age-old question faced again and again by football fans everywhere. Much respect goes to the Guy who can time and time again make the correct call, regardless of his loyalties to one team or another.

POP QUIZ

The word that is *not* banned on a job site is:

- **A.** nurture
- **B.** tender
- **C.** beer
- **D.** cute
- **E.** fabulous

Plausible Deniability on the Golf Course

When you step up to the tee, start making excuses before
you even hit your first shot, establishing plausible deniability.
Do not, especially on the first hole, make lofty claims of pro-
level performances or previous holes in one. Avoid giving
your buddies something to rub in your face later when you're
25 over par.

SIDEBAR

Plausible D, as it's known, applies to many other
aspects of Guy life. Take, for instance, computers.
Plausible D might sound like "Oh, I never worked with
this version of the program," or "You've got a Brand X
computer and I usually use a Brand Y." For scores of
men it is used as liberally as salt and pepper.

SIDEBAR

A good warm-up with a nice slow follow-through is a
great way to make the Guys think you know more
about this game than you do. A nice, slow stroke
that just grazes the ground is a great way to show
your "upcoming power" and is much better than a lip
flapping in the wind could ever be.

Striking Out in Baseball

After striking out in baseball, never look at the bat as if it could yield an answer to your blunder. You struck out. Face it. You'll just look silly staring at the bat after the fact. Walk back to the dugout in disgrace and buy the first round after the game.

SIDEBAR

If you do strike out, don't say a thing, just grab your glove and see if you can fill in for the first base coach. If not, then go sit alone and think about how you can drive the next pitch through the pitcher's mound.

POP QUIZ

Under no circumstances should you allow a woman to push the buttons for you on an elevator because:

A. after all, you're the man

B. chivalry is still alive and well

C. she may have done it wrong

D. this removes the chance of any preliminary check-out

Throwing Harder Than Is Necessary

During the game, a Guy is allowed to throw the ball much harder than is necessary after he just screwed up another play. It's his chance to show that he can at least throw the ball hard, even if he can't catch. When playing catch with your buddy, it is inevitable that one Guy will start the escalation of throwing harder than is necessary. This doesn't end until someone throws a wild one and the ball lands in the neighbor's yard.

SIDEBAR

 If you are going to engage in this tumultuous event, be sure to let the other Guys know that you have a cannon for an arm. Otherwise, the only thing you prove is that you have no accuracy and can throw a wild ball. Even girls can do that.

Warming Up with the Most Bats

Don't be the macho Guy at a baseball game who tries to swing the largest number of bats he can physically hold while warming up. Some Guys try to be like Mighty Casey on steroids in some neanderthal flashback. Remember you're there to hit the ball, not split a log.

SIDEBAR

There is no glory in tearing a rotator cuff or twisting your wrist off your arm just to warm up. Sometimes less really is more.

How might you redeem yourself after making a poor lumber selection at the store?

   A. recovering from a bent nail when hammering
   B. never running out of beer at the project site
   C. going back to the store for better lumber
   D. letting everyone give you a stiff verbal thrashing about your poor choice of lumber
   E. carrying all the heavy stuff yourself

GUY RULES

Chapter 9

Tools

GUY TOOLS

You must have the right tools for the job, or in Guy's terms, you gotta find the right job for the tools that you think are really cool. Why do we share this fascination with power tools? Why is ¼ HP better than ⅛ HP? What is HP? These questions and more we hope to answer in this chapter.

For starters, HP is the index used in "Guy" purchases to proclaim just how cool we think a tool is, as opposed to how much power is adequate for the job. The bigger the HPs, the better the "wow" factor is among our fellow Guys. A clear indication of that is when a Guy says, "Hey, I really got a thing for routers, so I got a huge one." But we at least have learned to pool our resources, in an effort to play with a variety of impressive power tools borrowed from the buddy network. It feels just as good to use your friend's 15 HP router as it would if it were yours. It also serves as good Guy-bonding material for idle talk about interesting projects, an honored pastime of ours.

The proficient use of these tools displayed on the work site is also an extremely important aspect of the whole tool experience. Proving to other Guys that we know what we're doing with this stuff is important to establish. No Guy likes to be looked down upon from Legos to Yugos. Maybe this should be part of ego. Then again, this entire book could be dedicated to ego, but that would be too egotistical.

Bending the Nail

You can recover from total failure in the lumber selection process and in the sawing of the wood if you can pull it all together with a good recovery of the nail. The ability to salvage a bent nail and drive it home establishes a Guy on a specific plane in project Guydom.

SIDEBAR

Every Guy respects a buddy who can take a seemingly unrecoverable nail and drive it home. On the other hand, every Guy hates the buddy who decides that he is going to drive that nail into the wood, regardless of how badly bent it is. This Guy will pull it out, straighten it five times, and still not get that nail into the wood. The only thing he will have to show for his hard work will be a worm-shaped nail driven into the side of the board so everyone can see it.

POP QUIZ

When you're on the freeway in your beater car, and a woman in a light blue minivan is about to pass you:

- **A.** let her go, you don't want to push your car
- **B.** cut her off to preserve your ego
- **C.** stop at nothing short of throwing a rod to prevent her from passing
- **D.** let her pass, but at least get a good scope of her as she goes by

Borrowing Tools

While you can't go borrow simple tools like a tape measure from the neighbor, it's perfectly acceptable to ask your neighbor to borrow a killer tool like his cement mixer or cherry picker. The time has come, and you finally have an opportunity to try out the heavy tools that for months you've watched him use with envy. Just make damn sure you know what you're doing, or you won't be borrowing that anymore because you'll own a broken one.

SIDEBAR

 Whatever you do, don't break it. Even if you go out and replace whatever it was that you broke, you still look like an idiot for breaking it. This is, in fact, one of the only times you can ask a buddy how a tool works. He'll be more than happy to tell you how it works and will appreciate you asking. On the other hand, you can't ask a Guy how a tool that you already own works because you look silly for owning one and not having a clue how to work it.

Figgerin'

When assembly is required, never read the assembly documentation. It always has big, concise, easy-to-understand pictures and diagrams to catch the rapid eye movement of men racing through manuals. The fine print is only for the second or third time redoing it because it doesn't work.

SIDEBAR

 Gant charts are the perfect example of this—big, colorful pictures with symbols and bars to look at when Guys intend to do some work.

POP QUIZ

Every Guy has needed a little help with the rug, but don't:

- **A.** ever use a permanent-wave gel
- **B.** get hair plugs
- **C.** stand in front of the mirror and pretend that you're some Hollywood stud-muffin
- **D.** use hair spray

Glove Envy

You must pay respect to the Guy with the time-worn, close-fitting, pocket-swelling, double-clutching, work gloves. Gloves that show clear evidence of hard work must be acknowledged by all the Guys present. Guys with no gloves, new gloves, or (in the worst case) gardening gloves don't have to go home, but they'd better be able to hammer a nail.

SIDEBAR

 Be sure to have at least one pair of gloves, no matter how old or feminine they may look. A pair of gloves is much better than no gloves. A real Guy doesn't mind upgrading his buddy with a better pair, but having no gloves is almost intolerable.

POP QUIZ

One of the two sets of directions that Guys give is:

A. the most efficient route
B. the one without stop lights
C. the one with the fewest left turns
D. you're-a-total-dumbass-if-you-can't-follow-these directions

Have Your Own Tools

Real Guys bring their own tools to the project. A Guy must be sure he has all his own tools, so he can compete and work right along with his buddies. If he doesn't, he'll end up being the gofer, or worse yet, forced to sit there and watch the real Guys work with their tools.

SIDEBAR

If the tool in question is specialized, like a wet saw, it's appropriate to pay the "tool boy" homage by humbly asking to borrow it.

SIDEBAR

This is especially true when it comes to the hammer, as nailing is the highest echelon in the order of things.

When stepping up to bat, it is imperative that you hit the bottom of your cleats, regardless of whether or not:

- **A.** you always strike out
- **B.** you know why you hit your cleats
- **C.** you have mud in them
- **D.** you even have cleats on

Power Tool Christening

When a Guy gets a new power tool it is a total breach of etiquette to even think about using it before he has. Of course, you'll never have to wait long, because the Guy will jump on the first opportunity to use it, even if it's totally inappropriate to the task at hand, like taking his new super-torque power drill to a dainty light fixture or his Chainsaw 3000 to his hedges. Feel honored when allowed to share in that moment, and understand that that's exactly how it has to happen within the natural order of things.

SIDEBAR

Be advised that Guys will be looking for any excuse to christen their new tool, even if it is a new drill press and the only way to use it is to lay the walls flat to drill holes for hanging pictures.

Ruler Freedom

Borrowing another Guy's tape measure for a project is like asking to borrow your buddy's penis for sex. Every Guy must have his own!

SIDEBAR

The competency of Guys is displayed through the use of tools they own. If a Guy doesn't even own the simplest of tools like a tape measure, he's most likely a cut-and-paste-with-construction-paper type of do-it-yourselfer.

POP QUIZ

When you're warming up for a football game with your buddies and one of them takes off and goes deep:

- **A.** throw it to someone else as a joke
- **B.** you are compelled to throw it to him just because he went deep
- **C.** overthrow him to force him to sprint so he doesn't go deep again
- **D.** fake it to him, then throw it away
- **E.** double-pump to throw off the other Guys

Sawing Excuse

When a Guy is doing a piss-poor job sawing and he makes the initial sawing excuse, his buddy must always check for corroborating evidence. If there's even a slight chance for plausible deniability, the excuse is valid. However, if it's revealed that the excuse, in fact, was not valid or, even worse, that he was an early-jumper-in Guy, then his buddy has a right to "slam him home."

| SIDEBAR |

You are advised that no Guy is compelled to let you off the hook for a poor sawing performance if after every time you push the saw through the blade flaps back and forth more than a flag at Arlington. You have to at least keep the thing moving smoothly through the cut to have any chance at plausible deniability.

POP QUIZ

When you're sitting next to another Guy and you encounter the "accidental" leg touch:

A. you make an adjustment to ensure that it doesn't happen again

B. do nothing and forget about it

C. demand to know just what the hell he thinks he's doing

D. tell all your buddies about it

Three Kinds of Hammering

Every Guy must be able to recognize the three levels of hammering skill. Each is more difficult to master than the previous one. (1) The cheesy Guy: choked up on the hammer, the mister-I'm-right-on-top-of-the-nail, laying-flooring kind of hammering. (2) The upright two-by-four style of hammering, like hanging a picture or shelves. (3) The kind that really separates the men from the boys is hanging drywall: nails in the mouth, leaning off the stepladder, back-breaking nailing. Respect must be shown to the hierarchy of hammering skill.

SIDEBAR

The real pro is truly poetry in motion. His ability to speak with a mouthful of nails is only matched by his ability to move objects with the hammer's claw.

Chapter 10
Wife

GUY WIFE

For fear of self-incrimination, it wouldn't be wise for us to elaborate too much on the introduction of this chapter. So, our poor judgment intact, we'll continue on with this preamble. The interaction we practice every day with the wife is often a dance with fate itself. We only hope to fumble our way through without being overly offensive. Mostly through misunderstanding (and sometimes through sports play-offs) our intentions are misread or misdirected, resulting in personal physical trauma.

Early Rejects

At the end of the night, don't forget to check your early rejects. Whether at the bar or on the project site, when you're getting down to the wire, be sure to look over the materials that you tossed aside at the beginning. When material is sparse, your early rejects can suddenly yield a crown jewel.

When you have a lot to choose from, your quality standards are very high. But when you get down to where the rubber hits the road, you will take just about anything to finish the job.

POP QUIZ

When your wife asks you if you love her while you are talking on the phone, she will wait for the:

- **A.** Guys to say something in the background
- **B.** coerced response
- **C.** the perfect time that all the Guys are listening
- **D.** the moment when you want to get off the phone the most

Fortune Cookie

When breaking up with a woman, *never* go to a Chinese restaurant to "talk things over." Even though you may successfully navigate through every painful passage of the meal, avoiding a scene, the fortune cookie will do you in.

SIDEBAR

Usually the fortune cookie says something like "You are surrounded by love and serenity." This does not support your case.

POP QUIZ

If you start the process of making the fire:

A. you must not stop short of using napalm to get it going

B. give your best effort, then turn it over to your buddy

C. you must take advice from your buddies

D. ask your wife for advice

E. use gas, it's easier

Guilt Tapestries

Some women work in guilt like others work in tapestries. A Guy puts up with guilt only as long as it provides him with a tactical trump card that he can use in the future.

 It is important to distinguish between guilt and an old-fashioned, and much needed, verbal lashing intended to keep you straight. Chances are that you have the lashing coming, but the guilt can be your savior later on.

POP QUIZ

Guys must attempt to subvert their women to mask their:

- **A.** need for a pack of smokes
- **B.** true purpose for going out to the store with their buddies
- **C.** absentmindedness
- **D.** project that just went bad

I Love You, Too

When a Guy is on the phone talking to his wife or girlfriend, and she knows he is sitting around with his buddies, she'll always throw out that "I love you," waiting for the coerced response. Buddies have to respect the Guy who can get away with "Me too" rather than the full-blown "I love you, too."

There is nothing worse than having to endure this treatment from your wife with the Guys sitting next to you. It is better to make a preemptive "I love you" than to have to react to the "Do you love me" assault. Give the short "I love you" first and every Guy there will know exactly what tactic you have employed.

When you're trying to trump another Guy's bullshit and it turns out that he is actually right:

- **A.** you had better say you're sorry
- **B.** you had better be able to explain why you said what you said
- **C.** you had better be able to take his comeback
- **D.** his bullshit stands and he earns the right to slam you home, either now or later.

Initial Eye Contact

Every Guy gets a little rattled when he makes the initial eye contact with a chick in a club. You must stay cool when your eyes meet. Never talk about it with your buddies until you have established a second confirmation contact. Only then can you mention it to the boys. If she catches you bragging on the *first* contact, you've blown your chances.

SIDEBAR

Only after a second contact can you even mention what has been going on with you and this woman. If she catches you freaking out on the first contact, you have blown your cool at the highest level.

POP QUIZ

When your buddy's wife calls him on the phone:

- **A.** you should listen in
- **B.** he must make his getaway so you don't hear
- **C.** make fun of how whipped he is
- **D.** yell excuses in the background, so his wife can hear, to help him get off the phone

Last Possible Moment

You've gotta wait until the last possible moment to tell your wife that you're going out with the Guys. Whether you're gonna play softball some night, going out drinking, or whatever, remember, you've gotta wait till the last moment to mention it to her. That way, while you'll still get your obligatory ration of shit, it will be for a much shorter period of time.

SIDEBAR

 Zen and the Art of Sneaking Out: Pretend that your wife really doesn't know what you're doing. Your wife, on the other hand, will normally let on that she's slightly upset because she knows exactly what game you're playing. You must show your buddies you're in control by sneaking out and joining them in activities that will most likely get you all in trouble. Only a few Guys choose to run with the pack.

SIDEBAR

 Guys will take the short, concentrated reminder of their violation of protocol over the long drawn-out rendition, which causes an onslaught of "speaker feedback."

Late to the Airport

When you're running late to the airport, you must stay cool. Assure all the parties involved that you know what you are doing. Use the following: "Don't worry, we have plenty of time, I got it handled, we're gonna make it." Even if you know deep down that it means you're gonna be runnin' over luggage in a full sprint to the gate.

Airport security delay: If you're late, you'll inevitably be stuck in the ultimate security delay with some Guy in front of you who's got the studded wrestling belt, steel-tipped boots, a big boom-box radio, and a parachute.

POP QUIZ

As long as the elastic is tight around your waist, then under no circumstances should you ever feel:

- **A.** compelled to discard your grundies
- **B.** that you have to buy new undershorts
- **C.** that you are getting too fat for your shorts
- **D.** as if you could be in an underwear commercial

Porn Test Fire

Every young Guy's got porno books stashed somewhere. If he's not sure his wife is cool with it, he'll leave one out to test the waters. If this "porn tracer" fails, he'll stash it like the wife does with her diary, because it contains his deepest thoughts and juiciest secrets.

SIDEBAR

If you are unsure of the outcome of this event, never use your most raunchy porn to test the waters. Start conservatively: If you can get a toehold you will have time to climb that next cliff.

POP QUIZ

When you're questioning your mechanic about your car repair, you must:

- **A.** act like you know more about it than he does
- **B.** try to bust him for double talking
- **C.** act like you know just what the heck he's talking about
- **D.** look to your wife for understanding

Sky Diving

If your wife or girlfriend decides that she wants to jump out of a plane, bungee jump, or some other crazy thing, you must participate as well. If you don't join her then you might as well put your penis in her purse, and hold it for her while she jumps.

SIDEBAR

There is some kind of "brave" instinct that's placed in the male psyche at an early age. Guys are exposed to comic-book heroes and plastic toy soldiers brave enough to face the onslaught of firecrackers and flamethrowers. Whatever it is, it denies us the ability to clearly see that jumping out of a perfectly good aircraft is just plain silly.

When you're working with other Guys on a project:

- **A.** be the survivor, not the hero: pace yourself and complete the project
- **B.** ridicule the older Guys for pacing themselves
- **C.** never be the first to call a break
- **D.** work as hard as you can right away to establish your dominance

Subversion

Guys must attempt to confuse their women to mask their true purpose for going out to the store with their buddies. Numerous "nonessentials" are used to veil the true reason for the work stoppage. They do this even though they know full well that the wife knows what they are really doing, since these nonsense items often end up resembling bottled beer.

SIDEBAR

 When you find that you need to duck out to the store with the boys for a second case of beer, you can use the time-tested ploy of acting like you are really upset that you have to leave. Uttering swear words under your breath, or complaining about how late in the day it is, are also good to use from time to time.

POP QUIZ

When a group of Guys are working together, who gets to call break time?

- **A** the youngest Guy
- **B.** the biggest whiner
- **C.** the Guy who is hosting the project
- **D.** whoever is first at it
- **E.** the oldest Guy

The Lump

No matter how sad the movie is that you've just watched, never shed a tear or allude to the fact that you've got a lump in your throat. Make fake adjustments and cover the evidence with snide and immature comments. Do whatever it takes to avoid emotional exposure. One tactic commonly employed is making fun of the wife's crying as a distraction while you get yourself under control. It was in an effort to avoid this phenomenon that the action flick was invented.

SIDEBAR

In order to prevent any chance that you will get sucked into this lump vortex at a movie, always protest going to any movie that could possibly bring on this dreaded event.

POP QUIZ

Guys can *never* be considered lost. They:

- **A.** are just looking for a place to purchase a map
- **B.** have just chosen to take an alternate route
- **C.** can always ask their wife
- **D.** drive around until they need gas
- **E.** send their girlfriend in to get directions

The Quick-Click Look

When a group of Guys are sitting around, the swift *rap-tap* of high heels on a hard surface beckons the "quick-click look." The Guy who can best pull off the "fake adjustment" verifies that it is indeed a female passing by, and not some Guy in fancy dress shoes. If he feels the woman is worthy of his buddies' attention, he must then signal them for the "sharing of the scope." They're counting on him.

SIDEBAR

Try to make the initial scan as discreetly as possible. It's very embarrassing to turn around and check out a Guy in dress shoes.

Final
Exam

1. **If you're doing something with a buddy that takes a particular skill, and you don't know what the hell you're doing, you:**

    A. ask for help
    B. mimic his actions
    C. blame it on your tools
    D. blame it on the beer

2. **When you're walking down the street with your wife or girlfriend, and you notice somebody else's construction project:**

    A. you have to say something nice about it
    B. you should ridicule the construction techniques
    C. just keep walking and don't bore her with the details
    D. you must comment on it and pretend like you know more than you do
    E. compare it to your last project

3. **When you're hanging out with your buddies, and you go to the fridge to get a beer:**

    A. go to the bathroom first
    B. wait until you get back to open it
    C. make the determination yourself as to who else needs one
    D. by god, get one for everyone

4. During the game, a Guy is allowed to throw the ball much harder than is necessary when:

A. proving he has a cannon for an arm

B. it's his chance to show that he can at least throw the ball hard, even if he can't catch

C. he is pissed off

D. he realizes the Guy catching it is a putz

5. Every Guy must be able to recognize the three levels of hammering skill as long as:

A. you know about hanging drywall with nails in your mouth

B. you are not the cheesy Guy

C. you are not having trouble hanging a picture

D. you didn't learn about it from Bob Villa

E. respect is shown for the echelon of hammering skill

6. Of the three types of campers, the one camper that doesn't need a tent is:

A. the self-contained-above-ground-moving camperatus

B. Mr. Let's-Go-Anywhere

C. the where-you-hang-a-ticket kind

D. the Guy who never goes camping

7. No matter how sad a movie is that you've just watched, if you feel the lump:

A. take a swig off your soda

B. ask your girlfriend to hand you the popcorn

C. point to any woman you see crying

D. cover the evidence with snide and immature comments

8. One of the two sets of directions that Guys give is:

A. to only tell the ones they know

B. the one without stoplights

C. the one with the fewest left turns

D. the "this-would-be-hard-for-somebody-else-to-find" directions

9. Guys must never reveal their *true* level of automotive knowledge, they should only:

A. repeat what their buddy said

B. listen for a weakness in their buddy's knowledge

C. wait for a safe opportunity to share

D. repeat what they have read

10. During the official introduction:

A. you must be willing to repeat your name twice

B. say "Nice to meet you."

C. you must introduce your wife

D. it is vital to shake hands with the other Guy

11. When is it okay to give your buddy unsolicited advice?

A. never, you must wait until he asks

B. if he's fumbling around

C. when you just can't stand to watch him screw up for one more second

D. when you know better than him

12. When is it time to back off on the smart-ass comments?

A. when you're being dangled by your feet off a bridge

B. before a fight breaks out

C. toward the end of the project

D. not until you take your last breath on this planet

13. If a Guy's really working hard, any good buddy will notice signs of fatigue and offer:

A. to get him a beer

B. to help, or even take over

C. to call a break

D. to be more supportive of his efforts

14. When you're physically carrying something heavy with a buddy, you have to be willing to carry your fair share of the load and act like:

A. you can't get a grip on the load

B. the load is not as heavy as it may appear

C. you have a bad back

D. you are the true beast of burden

15. When you eat at your buddy's house, should you rinse off your dishes?

A. yeah, right

B. what dishes?

C. more like chip off

D. only if he does

16. As packing czar, the Guy must be willing to bark orders to his minions, having them bring:

A. beer for as long as he is packing

B. every last piece of luggage and stage it in front of the car

C. the boxes first

D. the items in sequence according to his packing schema

17. When it's time to pay, never write a check; it's:

A. only the women who use those things

B. too hard to spell, anyway

C. strictly cash or credit

D. too hard to figure out the balance

18. When at a party and the pleasantries have been exchanged with other couples, a Guy must:

A. act like he likes his wife's friends

B. skillfully employ the art of ditching the wife

C. ask about the other couple's kids

D. put the beer they brought in the cooler

19. When your buddy shows up at the Halloween party in a sweaty, alien costume:

A. never let him live it down

B. you can't razz him because he's so sweaty and pathetic

C. knock his mask off his face

D. pretend like you don't know who it is

20. Stand by your critique of the pass reception; just make sure that:

A. you're right

B. you can back up your opinion with astute observations

C. you're the loudest when shouting out your opinion over everyone else

D. you cover yourself in case you're wrong

E. nobody else is going to contradict you, except the instant replay

21. When is it okay to borrow a Guy's new power tool?

A. when he is not sure how to use it and needs some nurturing from you

B. never, don't be ridiculous

C. if he got two new cool power tools at once

D. when you helped his wife pick it out for his birthday present

22. You are sitting with a group of Guys and you hear the rhythmic *tap* of high heels on a hard surface. After verification, you should . . .

A. enjoy what your buddies are missing

B. act suave and debonair, and, above all, look stately

C. discreetly alert your buddies to be sure not to miss anything

D. whistle and coo loudly like a complete idiot

23. What tool is it not okay to borrow from the buddy network of tools?

   A. cement mixer

   B. wet saw

   C. router

   D. tape measure

24. How do you hide the fact that you have a lump in your throat from the sad movie you're watching with your wife?

   A. turn your face away from your woman

   B. go get a beer from the fridge

   C. make fake adjustments

   D. leave the room, pretending like you have to go to the bathroom

   E. none of the above

25. Farting terms for Guys are just as important as:

   A. mortgage terms

   B. United Nations terms of protocol

   C. butt-sniffing terms for dogs

   D. cigars are to the president

Visit www.guyrules.com to join Club Guydom and see how others did on the exam.

Glossary

Accidental: That moment when you begin to wonder just what is going on, since lightning is never supposed to strike twice in the same place.

Acknowledge: To concede a bit of good performance on your buddy's part, letting him know that it was above his usual standard.

An out: Escape pod; safety line; cover.

Anticipation: When you find yourself flashing back to the moment when your buddy offered the contraband in the first place. You may find yourself waiting for the next possible moment to mention the "exchange" or rehearse how you are going to ask him to follow through with the agreement.

Artificial time frame: When pressure is placed upon you by an outsider who does not have to live with the mess. Offhanded comments that allude to your mess or nasty dish smell must never enter into a decision to clean up the mess. False guilt is also included in the process.

Automotive knowledge exposure: The dreaded, unintended event in which a Guy reveals his level of automotive knowledge, or more to the point, his lack of knowledge.

Bastion: A work projecting outward from the main enclosure of a fortification, consisting of two faces and two flanks, and so constructed that it is able to be defended by flanking fire.

Blue minivan: An American icon of freedom of choice gone sour.

Brand: Not only a brand name, but a kind of tool. Pliers versus Vise-Grips, or Macintosh over Windows. It can get ugly.

Breach of Guydom: When some action or event goes against the normal protocol, causing everything after to be dangerously out of control.

Bunch of crap: A collection of thoughts or ideas that go against your beliefs and are securely founded in Guydom.

By god: The inbred knowledge that if you don't do something, other Guys will forever remember your mistake. Forgiveness may be forthcoming, but forgetting would be almost unthinkable. Never tread in those murky waters.

Camperatus: The total concoction of camping gear that a Guy puts together in order to go camping. No two camperati are the same and must never be, since the camperatus is one of the true measures of Guydom.

Campfire: The ultimate symbol of a Guy's ability to do something wrought of pure Guydom. A Guy's ability to create one is a major indicator to his buddies of his level of manliness.

Choir boy: The Guy who can convince almost anyone that there could never be a moment when he would use any phrase stronger than "dang it" or "by golly."

Christen: Analogous to dogs marking their territory.

Cigar: Leisure product developed as an experiment to see how far to each end of loving something and hating something different people can be.

Clear evidence: Any visible sign of wear, paint stain, or holes worn into the fingers of work gloves. Faded leather is always a plus.

Clearance: The okay from the wife; never acknowledged in the presence of your buddies, always remains private.

Coerced response: Communication from Guy to woman, prompted by said woman, in an effort to reaffirm or prove the Guy's love for her.

Cologne: A smelly substance that a Guy applies to his face and neck in a vain effort to cover up his natural stink; see "fart."

Competency: A Guy's ability to play the project game with his buddies. Every Guy who is working on a project will at some point need all the other Guys to help him out of a jam. The ability to help out is a direct reflection of his competency.

Cool: Condition green; everything checks out between you and your woman; can often be deceiving and not actually real.

Corroborating evidence: Physical proof that supports a claim (usually in defense) of an event that on the surface seemed to go against Guydom but was actually caused by some force beyond control.

Crown jewel: The perfect thing that marks the end of a project. The one perfect thing you are looking for.

Czar: The final word on all matters related to the distribution and placement of any luggage for a trip. The final authority on packing. The all-knowing space miser, able to fit six square feet of luggage into three square feet of trunk space with precision.

Don't worry: This does not mean "Don't worry"; it means "Don't worry, I am busting my butt to cover for whatever mistake was made and caused us to be late." It is another way of saying "You had better hold on once we get into the car because all bets are off."

Driving situation: Any time that you find yourself having to take evasive action while driving. It is generally associated with a pounding heart, sweaty brow, and clammy hands. Always unintentional, never predicted.

Dumb Guy: The Guy that under normal circumstances performs feats of Guydom with distinction, yet at a specific moment does something so stupid that every Guy within sight or sound has no choice but to notice "said event." There can be no doubt that the action in question was a complete breach of etiquette.

Dye: Unknown throughout Guydom except in unfortunate, misguided exceptions.

Embellish: The art of not exactly lying, but not telling the entire truth about an event. It is an attempt to "clarify" events that may have been missed during the original event.

Envy: That feeling you get when you are pulling a sliver out of your hand and your buddy is continuing to work because he doesn't have wussy hands like you.

Fart: A primitive form of communication between Guys.

Fast food: Known to many as junk or chain food. Must contain massive quantities of grease or lard. Processed animal carcass is generally a staple. Served to customers through a small window where incompetent workers get the order wrong more often than not.

Fat: This term has no meaning on its own. It is completely relative, depending entirely on how the Guy perceives himself, or more importantly, what his buddies think of him. Four hundred pounds could just mean "solid," while a short, bald Guy who weighs 210 and never sticks up for himself is clearly "fat."

Fat Guy: That doughboy body that looks like an overfilled water bag.

First: The initial time you catch a woman looking at you. Chances are that it was, in fact, not the first time she has checked you out; however, it is the first time she let you see her checking you out. Subsequent check-outs depend on the way in which one handles this contact.

First opportunity: Acceptable use of the tool does not include cutting the box or drilling a hole in the Styrofoam container after opening it on Christmas Day. There must be a certifiable project in which the tool can be used (a contrived project is fine).

Flounder: The sweaty brow, wringing hands, and other agitated motions a Guy goes through while facing up to the fact that he screwed up.

Fuck with a Guy: To harass a Guy with sarcastic and smart remarks long enough to get him really irritated; watch out for payback time, because it will come.

Gauntlet: When you find yourself stuck between a person who forces the clerk to do a price check, and the person who starts unloading their cart "horn of plenty" before you get a chance to check out. The rubber divider is dropped with a thud before you can make your getaway.

Gets the axe: When a good Guy is expendable for financial reason beyond the control of the Work Gods. Generally, this is due to an upturn in Web traffic, which is stealing corporate profits.

Good hit: Usually referring to American football, though often to hockey as well, it describes the instant when contact between two players is so solidly made that you can hear the cracking sound and almost feel the hit.

Gofer: When a Guy is reduced to no real skilled labor of his own, but just goes for various supplies needed by the real Guys.

Grand Canyon: More than a place, it's an event. You may be playing basketball and find yourself blowing out a lung, breathing as if you were on Mount Everest. That is your personal Grand Canyon.

Grilldom: The domain of rituals associated with a grill, including equipment, protocol, burnt meat, and lots of lighter fluid. Related to "Kingdom."

GuyBond: That moment when a Guy shares something with you, which if you had shared with him, you would not want him telling anyone. This is such a big event that you don't even need to be told "That's between you and me." It's known.

Guydom: This whole book and the line of shameless merchandise that will follow it.

Half dead: The point at which a Guy finds himself ready to quit any project with little or no regard for protocol or consequence in the realm of Guydom.

Halloween: Meaning evolves with age: excuse to consume tons of candy; excuse to attend wild parties; any excuse to get out of the house for the night to avoid the visitors.

Hammering: The act of driving a nail into a chunk of wood. Not to be confused with the overconsumption of beer, although the two can be closely linked.

Handle-rattle-hose method: The technique employed at the gas pump by all Guys who, at the point when the gas flow stops automatically, squeeze the pump trigger a few times while vigorously shaking the pump handle, which is still inserted in the tank, in an effort to deposit every last drop of gas into the vehicle.

Hasty call: You jump in way too early on your call about how the play went down; risk of being wrong is too high to warrant this in most situations.

Hero to zero: That instant when a Guy tumbles from being the King of Now to the court jester of what could've been.

Hollywood stud-muffin: What you think you are when you are convinced that you are the best-looking Guy on the face of the earth. You may be having a particularly good hair day or you may be a little less fat for some reason.

Hostile beer takeover: The point at which you drool back enough fluid into the bottle that your buddy no longer wants it back.

In disgrace: That moment when you have to walk back to the dugout and prepare to listen to your buddies talk about what you just did. If a player is a good player, he can expect to have his boys toss him a bone, but if he sucks, he knows he may get the cold shoulder. The darkest of moments in a player's career.

In tune with the ways of Guydom: When you're aligned so perfectly with the unspoken protocol between Guys that you'd embarrass construction workers.

Inevitable: What it is when one Guy fires a ball past another Guy waiting to receive it. Guys who do this inevitably end up playing catch by themselves.

Insider trading details: The "top secret" information about where he got the best deal on any building materials. For example, the location of the lowest-cost rental equipment store in town or the name of the Guy who loaned him his truck and trailer.

Is: That depends on what you mean by "is."

Killer tool: One of the biggest pieces of hardware you have ever used. The kind of tool where you ask the kids to stand back, because legends have been created involving the use of this tool.

Kingdom: The illusion of control that you maintain over your wife or children. Chances are that you are, in fact, in control as long as your wife allows it.

Last possible: The moment when you know that, while time would allow for more delay, any further lateness will involve crossing over all reasonable marriage rules and could spell destruction of your plans.

Light-brush-bead-sweat: The slight sheen of sweat that instantly forms on a Guy's brow one second after the instant that light, brushing contact is made with his most sensitive area.

Looking cool: This relative baseball term really means looking cool for your own sake, since the only thing that spectators care about is if you can hit the ball or not.

Lump vortex: That point in time where no matter what ploy you try, you can not fight off the lump and you find yourself spiraling directly into a pond of glassy eyes.

Macho: The Guy who has the little-man complex and thinks he can convince everyone that he really is a strong Guy, even if he can't hit the ball out of the infield.

Material is sparse: When you have a need for something and you only have it in small quantity. Generally, there is little chance of getting more of it.

Memorize: The ability to effectively fumble your way through any complicated setup.

Merging bone: Used when you recognize that the Guy next to you is desperate to get into the flow of traffic, seconds from that critical moment when he either runs off the road, stops, or forces his way into your lane.

Mimic-when-unsure ploy: Involves fake adjustments, distracting movements, or any other activity with the purpose of delaying action until the required moves can be observed, then emulated.

Mistake: Any unforeseen obstacle in the way of success that can, in some way, be blamed on anyone or any object.

Mr. Drop-It: Drops a tool or piece of unused material wherever it ceases to be useful to him.

Mr. Happy: Your own pet name for "it."

Mr. Peg-Board: Feels anxious until each tool is wiped down and placed back in its appropriate spot on the Peg-Board, indicated by its distinct outline painstakingly redrawn each season by hand.

Neanderthal flashback: When a Guy suddenly loses his finer sense of modern protocol and reverts back to his most basic instincts; those animal urges that lie beneath the surface of everything a Guy does.

Never: Never does not mean you never get lost, it only means never when others, particularly your wife, are in the car with you. If you are in the vehicle alone, you're lost when you're lost.

New grip: That adjustment where you appear to be finding a better place to hang on to some object while carrying it, but really you're just buying yourself some time. It is important to add a slight bounce or movement to show that you are making the adjustment.

Nonessential: Any item that your wife asks you to pick up while you are at the store, saving her a trip. Closely related to brownie points.

Official introduction: When someone either introduces you to another Guy, or one Guy asks another Guy what his name is during conversation.

Other Guy's benefit: Washing your hands better than you would normally to prove to the other Guy that you take hygiene very seriously. Some Guys wash their hands so well when other Guys are around that they could almost go into surgery.

Participate: The ability to act as if you are enjoying everything that your wife is doing. Acting as if you had wanted to do whatever you are doing out of pride and ego is a must. You are normally just there to participate.

Party Guy: A dude you may or may not know, but whom you party with so suddenly he's cool in your book.

Pecking order: The organization of Guys by how much respect is won, often based on one's ability to talk the talk.

Pet talk: The affectionate banter of pet owner to pet. Sometimes it is hard to tell which is the pet and who owns whom.

Pizza: One of the major food groups; known to sustain a Guy for over a year straight.

Pizzazz: A word that (verified through scientific documentation) is used no more than three times in the life expectancy of the modern male.

Poor-lumber-selection excuse: Employed when the project goes bad and you need something to blame; it's often difficult to verify one way or another if it really was the poor lumber that caused the problem.

Porn tracer: The act of testing the reaction to the introduction of pornography into the relationship. Like a red tracer round fired by an M-16 at night, the porn tracer will land with a solid blow or ricochet into the darkness, never to be seen again.

Post facto: When you know you are safe and out of danger of crashing because your buddy was driving way too fast.

Primeval Guydom: The set of rules that bound the social behavior of primitive man. Rules from this set that still apply today are considered the most rudimentary, and indeed, the most deeply ingrained rules in male genetic coding.

Project Guydom: Any project in which Guys are involved. Characteristically, the "home owner" will have planned the project, purchased the materials, rounded up his circle of Guys, and prevented any disruption by the female species, allowing for an uninterrupted project.

Prove: Living up to all requirements that indicate a Guy is in fact not "whipped" or under the control of his wife. There is no evidence that this Guy's wife would ever house his penis in her purse.

Purchase approval: The acknowledgment from your buddy that the latest gadget you bought is worthy of Guydom.

Quality Guy: The Guy who never fails to impress you with his thoroughness and attention to minute detail; it may take him ten times as long to finish anything than a hasty Guy, but the end result shows it (it's just five years out of style already).

Quick-click: That rhythmic tapping of high heels on a hard surface that you turn your head to see.

Rapid eye movement: The equivalent of Evelyn Wood speed reading for understanding directions.

Real beer: The beer that, for some reason, you have to use a bottle opener on in order to drink it. When you take a cheap, piece of trash beer and make a Guy use a bottle opener, it now becomes a microbrew. What gives?

Reluctant virgin: The Guy who protests just a little too much, making what on the surface seem to be reasonable excuses for not drinking, only to cave in to the "pressure" just before everyone accepts his excuses as factual and sound.

Ritual: Protocol followed by Guys, usually without them being aware of it; often trivial on the outside, but actually full of complexities that aren't completely understood or visible to the naked eye.

Rotting shirt: That constant smell that never stops stinking.

Ruin it yourself: When a simple job spins out of control, landing in the costly ditch of destruction. There is no financial solace in this type of project.

Saleswoman: The female sales consultant who is far too good looking for your own good. You will, in fact, know that you are acting irrationally and should just calm down and think about the purchase, but you're having trouble focusing.

Salvage: The ability to drive a nail into a piece of wood, once it has been bent because you hit the corner of the nail. This happens because you suck at nailing. Seldom is the problem a direct result of a knot in the wood.

Self-imposed pressure: Stress caused by your making lofty claims about new gear, your capabilities, making a deadline, how far you can run, or anything else that suddenly you're faced with the opportunity of proving.

Shaking up the entire balance of Guydom: Doing something that causes protocol to fall away and that forces Guys to suddenly act from pure instinct alone, quite often resulting in somebody getting hurt.

Sharing of the fat: When one Guy embellishes how fat he is to another Guy who is complaining about his own weight, even to the point of grabbing a handful and displaying it in an effort to somehow reassure him.

Skid marks: Those telltale lines that prove extracurricular gaseous activity. No Guy would ever admit to having such residue around women.

Slam home: To emphasize and articulate a distinct law of Guydom. This is often employed when a buddy hassles you over a break in etiquette, then later breaks the same rule himself, thus inviting you to give back what you have received: to slam it home.

Sniff test: Sticking dirty clothes into your face, inhaling, and taking a deep breath to determine if you can wear your clothes just one more day. Your standards will shift depending upon what activity you will be doing. Working out in the yard will have a much lower standard than going to work on a Friday.

Spell of a woman: When a Guy's instincts are suppressed, and suddenly he's thinking about words that are banned on the project site.

Starting: The act of engaging the starter while the engine is running in an effort to use a mechanical tool to point out your personal moment of stupidity.

Stupid diagnostic: The ability to figure something out if just left alone. This skill involves trying something over and over until the "thing" just ends up working and you look like a hero.

Surf: Wander; tied directly to man's attention span.

Swill: Whatever vile concoction your buddy brings along on the camping trip.

Switching: Having, as a result of circumstance, to force your taste buds to adjust to new stimuli. In short, drinking cheap beer.

Tactical trump card: A specific advantage that a Guy must use before its expiration date, which is fairly earned in a situation where said Guy won a strategic battle of protocol with either his buddies or his wife.

Talk things over: When you have avoided the separation conversation as long as possible and now the time has

arrived to have "it." The outcome of this dreaded event is usually already decided, but the execution of the conversation is what is always in question.

Testosterone: One of the three pillars of the triangle of Guydom, along with ego and instinct.

The slip: That moment when your wife realizes that you are not coming back. She should give some consideration to finding a group of people to talk to for a while.

Theory: The clear understanding of how to do something without having ever tested your idea. The implementation of your theory will be a perfect excuse to make fifteen trips to the hardware store in order to support your concept. However, you must find some excuse for why the brilliant plan failed, just before you abandon it and ask for help.

Threading the parking needle: Displays of parking nerve such as whipping into a tight spot too fast, performing a reverse park, or best of all, squeezing into a parallel park that nobody thought you'd manage.

Throwing the whole project into chaos: The process of making what was once a productive, smooth project into a stalled, off-track, seemingly endless mess.

Time-out: Taken by any Guy or group of Guys to send the message that time is being taken to carefully plan the next moves, when in fact time is being taken to desperately grasp how the hell they're going to get out of this mess.

Token protest: The protest that you use for a future time when you become completely disgusted with listening to your buddy's tunes. You may even instigate a small skirmish in the war over the music. This gives you leverage because you have the "I warned you" defense.

Total dumbass: This is a Guy who may very well be one of the brightest people you know, but for some reason, does something that is so stupid that even he can't defend it.

Traffic jam: Better known as a dead stop. Exhaust-smelling, engine-heating, temper-flaring traffic.

True measure of Guydom: An object (e.g., power tool), activity (e.g., making a fire), skill (e.g., crushing a beer can perfectly with your boot), or situation (e.g., landing the airplane because there's nobody else left alive to do it) by which Guys rate one another.

Trump: The act of metaphorically slamming your piece of information on your buddy's BS table in an attempt to prove that what he is saying is a bunch of crap.

Trump attempt: The time when a buddy is convinced he has you cornered in a BS story but the story in question is 100 percent accurate and verifiable.

Trumping: Overcoming; achieving an end to a more precise and accurate extent than the other Guy.

Truth: Perception.

Upcoming power: The amount of force you can put behind your driver just before you grab a wad of dirt and send it halfway down the fairway. In every case this dirt wad will beat the distance that the ball travels by ten yards after accounting for the massive slice.

Vicarious: Sure, whatever you say, pal.

Weak moment of hope: A moment of weakness when a Guy forgets what's real and allows himself the luxury of a quick self-deception.

Work ploy: Your top-secret technique that you use to trick a Guy into doing something he may (under normal circumstances) not do. This is used in order to turn the tables on him so he does exactly what you want him to do.

Worst fashion: You can't get any lower unless it is the queen mother.

Wuss: The state of being a Guy finds himself in when he's being ridiculed by his buddies for being, well, less than a Guy should be.

Answers to Individual
Pop Quiz Questions

Rule: **Blue Minivan Pass**
Pop Quiz: When someone from your buddy's team receives a good hit from your team, you:
Correct Answer: C

Rule: **Different Sets of Directions**
Pop Quiz: The true master of the TV channel-surf is the Guy who can flash back to his show:
Correct Answer: D

Rule: **Driver Controls the Music**
Pop Quiz: Initiating the hello when you're walkin' past a Guy on the sidewalk is:
Correct Answer: C

Rule: **Driving with Fast Food**
Pop Quiz: Each major piece of clothing must pass:
Correct Answer: C

Rule: Grinding the Gears
Pop Quiz: When talking to your pets with your buddies around, you should:
Correct Answer: B

Rule: Hands off the Environment
Pop Quiz: When a bachelor leaves his clothes in the washer too long, and his shirts develop a musty smell, he cannot:
Correct Answer: A

Rule: How Fast?
Pop Quiz: When you go to break up with a woman, where should you *not* do it?
Correct Answer: C

Rule: Jockey for Position
Pop Quiz: Why would you get demoted to gofer on a project?
Correct Answer: B

Rule: Let Him In
Pop Quiz: Every time you finish a large home-improvement project, it's imperative that you:
Correct Answer: D

Rule: Motorcycles and New Vehicles
Pop Quiz: Every Guy has his "I-beat-the-sales-Guy" story when he buys a truck or car, but he will never:
Correct Answer: C

Rule: On Pumping Gas
Pop Quiz: Every Guy must laugh when his buddy gets hit in the testicles because:
Correct Answer: A

Rule: Parking
Pop Quiz: When your buddy asks if you got laid on your date:
Correct Answer: E

Rule: Talking to the Mechanic
Pop Quiz: You've gotta wear your most expensive, very special cologne:
Correct Answer: A

Rule: Unintentional Start
Pop Quiz: Why do you mismatch your plates when your buddy comes over for dinner?
Correct Answer: B

Rule: You Didn't Really Almost Get into an Accident
Pop Quiz: When a project goes bad, every Guy must:
Correct Answer: A

Rule: Acknowledging a Good Toss
Pop Quiz: If your wife or girlfriend decides that she wants to jump out of a plane, bungee jump, or some other crazy thing:
Correct Answer: D

Rule: Cigars: The Ultimate Guy Occasion
Pop Quiz: When "assembly required" comes up in a new purchase, what should you do?
Correct Answer: A

Rule: Did You Get Laid?
Pop Quiz: When secretly rating another Guy on his lumber selection:
Correct Answer: D

Rule: Different Good-byes
Pop Quiz: When eating fast food and driving, the Guy riding shotgun is responsible for:
Correct Answer: A

Rule: Giving Your Buddy an Out
Pop Quiz: Starting a fire today is a return to primeval Guydom because:
Correct Answer: B

Rule: Guy Scar-Offs
Pop Quiz: If you're going to take a drink off your buddy's beer, you must:
Correct Answer: B

Rule: Helping Your Buddy Leave
Pop Quiz: If your buddy is complaining about his weight, you can make him feel better by:
Correct Answer: C

Rule: I Beat the Sales Guy
Pop Quiz: If you're going out with the boys, tell the wife:
Correct Answer: C

Rule: Introducing a Buddy to New Terminology
Pop Quiz: When is it acceptable to fart in another Guy's car?
Correct Answer: C

Rule: Listening In
Pop Quiz: If a Guy isn't sure his woman is cool with him having porn, he must:
Correct Answer: D

Rule: **Most Famous Person**
Pop Quiz: When you are driving and another Guy needs to merge into your lane, don't:
Correct Answer: C

Rule: **Porn Anticipation**
Pop Quiz: If you promise your buddy that you'll bring over new porn for him to borrow the weekend his wife is away:
Correct Answer: C

Rule: **Reacting to Your Buddy Getting Hit in the Nuts**
Pop Quiz: When you're drinking the hard stuff and it hits you wrong:
Correct Answer: D

Rule: **She's Cool with It**
Pop Quiz: When a Guy realizes another Guy is talking a bunch of crap, it's acceptable to:
Correct Answer: B

Rule: **Initiating the Hello**
Pop Quiz: Your buddy's better off making a pass at your wife than firing up your grill:
Correct Answer: A

Rule: **Armrest Control in the Movie Theater**
Pop Quiz: The lowest echelon of burp is done by the guy who sucks air into his gut and:
Correct Answer: D

Rule: **Cling-Ons**
Pop Quiz: When you buy new gear for that competitive sport you play with your buddies:
Correct Answer: D

Rule: Do It Yourself!
Pop Quiz: When you're hanging around your buddy's house, should you adjust his stereo?
Correct Answer: D

Rule: Elevator Buttons
Pop Quiz: Some Guys might try to be like Mighty Casey on steroids in some:
Correct Answer: A

Rule: Every Guy Has a Get-Rich Scheme
Pop Quiz: As with the "longest-fish story," your "how fast" speed will increase as:
Correct Answer: A

Rule: Fat Etiquette
Pop Quiz: If you decide to dye your hair blond, you should:
Correct Answer: D

Rule: Fight Embellishment
Pop Quiz: If you notice a Guy giving you signals that he's tired:
Correct Answer: D

Rule: I Know I'm Really Fat When...
Pop Quiz: How can you totally recover after a poor performance sawing some wood?
Correct Answer: A

Rule: Speak Up
Pop Quiz: You must know the difference between "do it yourself" and:
Correct Answer: C

Rule: Swimming Pool Rules

Pop Quiz: What isn't looked upon favorably by your buddies when swapping "most famous person I've ever met" stories?

Correct Answer: D

Rule: The Leg Touch

Pop Quiz: When a Guy gets out of the water, it is vital that he pull the bathing suit away from his now shrunken crotch unless:

Correct Answer: B

Rule: You're *Never* Lost

Pop Quiz: Man and machine are most at one when moving less than five miles an hour, and nowhere is this more apparent than:

Correct Answer: C

Rule: Bachelor Dishes

Pop Quiz: If your wife doesn't like you to party, what do you tell your partying friends?

Correct Answer: B

Rule: Christen the Toilet

Pop Quiz: If the driver has the vents pointed toward him, and he knows it, and he doesn't give it up:

Correct Answer: D

Rule: Commitment to Making the Fire

Pop Quiz: Never eat the last piece of pizza because:

Correct Answer: A

Rule: Controlling Your Grill

Pop Quiz: If you're a passenger in your buddy's car and a good song comes on the radio, what do you do?

Correct Answer: C

Rule: Drinking the Hard Stuff
Pop Quiz: When you're playin' basketball, it's quite acceptable to:
Correct Answer: C

Rule: Fire Is Really Important to Guys
Pop Quiz: When you're running late to the airport, you must:
Correct Answer: B

Rule: Grocery Cart Selection
Pop Quiz: Especially when working together on a project, each Guy will have:
Correct Answer: C

Rule: Initial Tent Setup
Pop Quiz: The Guy with the ugliest scar coupled with the most grotesque story will:
Correct Answer: D

Rule: Internal Surf Clock
Pop Quiz: If you're the type of Guy who leaves tools and materials lying all over the site until the end of the day, but your host is the type of Guy who picks things up along the way, you:
Correct Answer: D

Rule: Knob Faux Pas
Pop Quiz: When you make eye contact with a woman in a club, you must do the following before bragging to the boys:
Correct Answer: B

Rule: Mismatching the Plates
Pop Quiz: If you grind a gear:
Correct Answer: D

Rule: Pet Talk
Pop Quiz: If you're working on a project, and your book editor gets laid off due to a new corporate outlook:
Correct Answer: D

Rule: The Garage Is Your Kingdom
Pop Quiz: When is it okay to call pass interference when watching a football game?
Correct Answer: B

Rule: Blonds
Pop Quiz: You're at the gas station filling up the cruiser. The pump stops at the desired amount but:
Correct Answer: C

Rule: Brief Elasticity
Pop Quiz: While at the movies, and sitting next to some other Guy:
Correct Answer: C

Rule: Cleanest Pair of Dirty Clothes
Pop Quiz: The "fat-Guy" rule states that you're supposed to, as the years go on:
Correct Answer: D

Rule: Cologne Signification
Pop Quiz: When you step up to the tee, start making excuses before you even hit your first shot:
Correct Answer: C

Rule: Grading Farts
Pop Quiz: Being outwardly comfortable with a big, stinky weed hanging out of your face is:
Correct Answer: A

Rule: Hair Dryer
Pop Quiz: When at the grocery store and you need a cart for the weekly catch:
Correct Answer: C

Rule: Matching Clothes
Pop Quiz: Short of grinding your gears, there is no worse automotive offense than:
Correct Answer: A

Rule: Musty Shirts
Pop Quiz: When you have the perfect get-rich scheme:
Correct Answer: D

Rule: Sharing the Fart
Pop Quiz: When your buddy gets a new vehicle:
Correct Answer: C

Rule: Ultimate Burp
Pop Quiz: Guys are more stubborn than stupid, so to show what they can do, they must:
Correct Answer: A

Rule: Washing Your Hands in the Men's Room
Pop Quiz: After striking out in baseball never:
Correct Answer: B

Rule: Backsplash
Pop Quiz: A true pro can tell his story about a fight so well that he can proclaim:
Correct Answer: B

Rule: Crushing the Can

Pop Quiz: When you're working with a buddy and it comes to the point when you know he screwed up, and he knows he screwed up, you must:

Correct Answer: B

Rule: Don't Eat the Last Piece

Pop Quiz: Finishing first is a bonus, but:

Correct Answer: B

Rule: Teeth and Beer

Pop Quiz: You're compelled to call out when your team should take a time-out, but always avoid:

Correct Answer: C

Rule: That First Beer

Pop Quiz: If a Guy's buddies are coming over to help on a project, it is completely inappropriate to offer beer in glass bottles because:

Correct Answer: D

Rule: The Big Switch

Pop Quiz: When the Guy next to you farts, you must:

Correct Answer: C

Rule: The Trump Goes Bad

Pop Quiz: When a Guy throws something to you exceptionally well you must:

Correct Answer: C

Rule: Trumping the Bullshit

Pop Quiz: The hand-washing ritual will become more vigorous for:

Correct Answer: A

Rule: Degrees of Vulgarity
Pop Quiz: The only time you are allowed to use the directions for setting up your tent is:
Correct Answer: C

Rule: Editor Gets the Axe
Pop Quiz: Only wash your dishes when the smell is so bad you can't stand it, or:
Correct Answer: D

Rule: Half Your Time
Pop Quiz: Avoid at all costs entering into a repair project with:
Correct Answer: C

Rule: Hasty Quality?
Pop Quiz: It is quite acceptable to make eye contact with another Guy during a good-bye:
Correct Answer: B

Rule: Know When to Call the Expert
Pop Quiz: When in the midst of a project and it's come to the dreaded moment of switching beer brands:
Correct Answer: D

Rule: Let's Call It a Day
Pop Quiz: At the end of the night, don't forget to check:
Correct Answer: C

Rule: Lumber Selection
Pop Quiz: When hanging out with a buddy at your place, you must be willing to help him leave, so he can:
Correct Answer: A

Rule: Project Goes Bad
Pop Quiz: If your wife stops you from leaving the house because your clothes don't match:
Correct Answer: A

Rule: Project with Your Wife
Pop Quiz: If you find yourself in a "driving situation" in which you know you just barely escaped an accident, you must hope to:
Correct Answer: C

Rule: Showing Off the Project
Pop Quiz: Vulgarity is inversely proportional to:
Correct Answer: D

Rule: Taking Breaks
Pop Quiz: When a Guy on the project has a pair of time-worn work gloves:
Correct Answer: D

Rule: Two Types of Building Guys
Pop Quiz: When stuck in traffic:
Correct Answer: A

Rule: Words That Are Banned on the Project Site
Pop Quiz: When you're working on a project with a group of Guys, when do you offer that first beer?
Correct Answer: D

Rule: Working Longer
Pop Quiz: A Guy puts up with the guilt only as long as:
Correct Answer: A

Rule: Caution: Pass Interference
Pop Quiz: When is it acceptable to use the new toilet in your buddy's new place when you're helping him move in?
Correct Answer: C

Rule: Commentary Time-Out
Pop Quiz: Should you validate a Guy's new terminology when he's sharing it with you?
Correct Answer: A

Rule: Exaggerated Foul
Pop Quiz: Every Guy must establish control over:
Correct Answer: C

Rule: Going Deep
Pop Quiz: When at the swimming pool, there's a feeling of "shirt peer pressure" that compels every Guy to:
Correct Answer: D

Rule: Hitting the Bottoms of your Cleats
Pop Quiz: Every Guy must be a virtual MacGuyver of:
Correct Answer: C

Rule: New Gear Expectations
Pop Quiz: What helps establish you in the classroom pecking order?
Correct Answer: C

Rule: Nice Hit!
Pop Quiz: What Guy possession are you expressly forbidden to borrow?
Correct Answer: D

Rule: Pass Reception Critique
Pop Quiz: The word that is *not* banned on a job site is:
Correct Answer: C

Rule: Striking Out in Baseball
Pop Quiz: Under no circumstances should you allow a woman to push the buttons for you on an elevator because:
Correct Answer: D

Rule: Warming Up with the Most Bats
Pop Quiz: How might you redeem yourself after making a poor lumber selection at the store?
Correct Answer: A

Rule: Bending the Nail
Pop Quiz: When you're on the freeway in your beater car, and a woman in a light blue minivan is about to pass you:
Correct Answer: C

Rule: Figgerin'
Pop Quiz: Every Guy has needed a little help with the rug, but don't:
Correct Answer: C

Rule: Glove Envy
Pop Quiz: One of the two sets of directions that Guys give is:
Correct Answer: D

Rule: Have Your Own Tools
Pop Quiz: When stepping up to bat, it is imperative that you hit the bottom of your cleats, regardless of whether or not:
Correct Answer: C

Rule: Ruler Freedom
Pop Quiz: When you're warming up for a football game with your buddies and one of them takes off and goes deep:
Correct Answer: B

Rule: Sawing Excuse
Pop Quiz: When you're sitting next to another Guy and you encounter the "accidental" leg touch:
Correct Answer: A

Rule: Early Rejects
Pop Quiz: When your wife asks you if you love her while you are talking on the phone, she will wait for the:
Correct Answer: B

Rule: Fortune Cookie
Pop Quiz: If you start the process of making the fire:
Correct Answer: A

Rule: Guilt Tapestries
Pop Quiz: Guys must attempt to subvert their women to mask their:
Correct Answer: B

Rule: I Love You, Too
Pop Quiz: When you're trying to trump another Guy's bull-shit and it turns out that he is actually right:
Correct Answer: D

Rule: Initial Eye Contact
Pop Quiz: When your buddy's wife calls him on the phone:
Correct Answer: B

Rule: Late to the Airport
Pop Quiz: As long as the elastic is tight around your waist, then under no circumstances should you ever feel:
Correct Answer: A

Rule: Porn Test Fire
Pop Quiz: When you're questioning the mechanic about your car repair, you must:
Correct Answer: C

Rule: Sky Diving
Pop Quiz: When you're working with other Guys on a project:
Correct Answer: A

Rule: Subversion
Pop Quiz: When a group of Guys are working together, who gets to call break time?
Correct Answer: E

Rule: The Lump
Pop Quiz: Guys can *never* be considered lost. They:
Correct Answer: B